DECORATING COOKIES PARTY

50 *Designs* FOR GUESTS TO *Make* OR *Take*

Bridget Edwards

LARK

LARK

An Imprint of Sterling Publishing
387 Park Avenue South
New York, NY 10016

Text and how-to photography © 2014 by Bridget Edwards

Project photography on pages 34, 46, 56–57, 68–69, 76, 88, 102, 112–113, 124, 132 © 2014 by Lark Books, an Imprint of Sterling Publishing Co., Inc.

ISBN 978-1-4547-0868-1

Library of Congress Cataloging-in-Publication Data

Edwards, Bridget, author.
  Decorating cookies party / Bridget Edwards.
    pages cm
  Includes index.
  ISBN 978-1-4547-0868-1
  1. Cookies. 2. Sugar art. 3. Icings (Confectionery) I. Title.
  TX772.E334 2014
  641.86'54--dc23
                              2013043170

Distributed in Canada by Sterling Publishing
c/o Canadian Manda Group, 165 Dufferin Street
Toronto, Ontario, Canada M6K 3H6
Distributed in the United Kingdom by GMC Distribution Services
Castle Place, 166 High Street, Lewes, East Sussex, England BN7 1XU
Distributed in Australia by Capricorn Link (Australia) Pty. Ltd.
P.O. Box 704, Windsor, NSW 2756, Australia

For information about custom editions, special sales, and premium and corporate purchases, please contact Sterling Special Sales at 800-805-5489 or specialsales@sterlingpublishing.com.

Email academic@larkbooks.com for information about desk and examination copies. The complete policy can be found at larkcrafts.com.

Every effort has been made to ensure that all the information in this book is accurate. However, due to differing conditions, tools, and individual skills, the publisher cannot be responsible for any injuries, losses, and other damages that may result from the use of the information in this book.

Manufactured in China

2 4 6 8 10 9 7 5 3 1

larkcrafts.com

CONTENTS

COOKIE DECORATING BASICS

THE PROJECTS

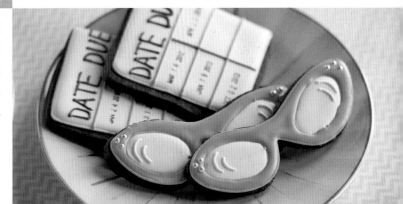

Introduction

Cookies love a party! It's true. Cookies are the perfect treat for just about any sort of celebration and are almost impossible to refuse. You may see someone turn down a slice of cake, but a cookie? Never! Who can resist just one?

In this book, we'll be talking cookie parties! Whether you want to make a platter of cookies to bring to a celebration, or you're hosting a cookie decorating party of your own, you'll find tips, tricks, and recipes to guide you on your way. As much as I love a cookie party for one (as in pajamas, cookie, cappuccino), I think cookies are best when shared.

More than 15 years ago, I decided to try my hand at decorating cookies. Armed with sugar, flour, and a husband willing to eat lots of mistakes, I taught myself via trial and error (lots of error). In 2007, I started my blog, Bake at 350, to teach others what I learned, and continue to learn to this day, about decorating cookies.

Flip through these pages, and you'll find cookie themes for book club parties, tailgate parties, and, oh yes, princess parties. If you love an entire set of cookies, make them all! If you want to make just one design, that's perfectly okay, too. We'll talk about hosting cookie-decorating parties and decorating cookies with kids (bring your patience). We'll play with stamping, double-decker cookies, and disco dust, too. I'm also thrilled to share with you some new cut-out cookie recipes (hello, mocha and gluten-free), along with my tried-and-true favorite sugar-cookie recipe.

Most importantly, I want you to have fun! One of my favorite home bloggers, The Nester of Nesting Place, has a saying: "It doesn't have to be perfect to be beautiful." That goes for cookies, too. They aren't meant to be perfect—they're meant to be shared...and eaten.

Are you ready for a cookie party? Let's get started!

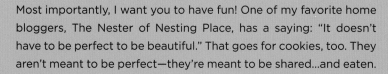

COOKIE DECORATING BASICS

Equipment

To make the simple recipes in this book, you'll need a few kitchen gadgets and some baking supplies. You probably have these items in your pantry right now. If not, then go ahead and gather the items listed on the following pages and prepare yourself for a cookie party!

Stand Mixer

Whether you're beating stiff cookie dough or whipping icing for 10 minutes, you'll find that a stand mixer is invaluable. It isn't essential for making cookies, but I can't imagine my kitchen without one. You can use the paddle attachment that comes with the mixer for icing and for dough—you don't need to buy a specialty scraper blade.

Cookie Cutters and Templates

It almost goes without saying that you'll need a few cookie cutters when you start baking. Tin, copper, plastic—any kind will work. You can find them in craft stores, at the supermarket, and in kitchen supply shops. There are lots of cookie cutter shops online, too. I've listed my favorites in the Resources section on page 144.

If you have a cookie idea but can't find the perfect cutter, then try using a template. Most of the shapes in this book are made with cookie cutters, but a few of them come from templates, which you'll find on page 143. All you have to do is trace the design onto a piece of cardstock and cut it out. If you want to make a washable, multi-use template, then trace your design on a sheet of plastic designed for making quilt templates.

To use a template, place it directly on top of your rolled-out cookie dough and cut around it with a paring knife. The edges won't be as sharp and crisp as those cut with a cookie cutter, so you'll need to smooth them a bit with your finger before baking.

Icing Tips and Couplers

Most basic cookie decorating can be done with just a few plain tips. My go-to tips for outlining are plain #2 and #3. I use #1 when adding small details. In this book, we'll also play with specialty tips like the petal, the leaf, and the star.

Tips are inexpensive and fun to have in the kitchen on those days when you want to play around with your icing. I have multiples of the tips that I use the most often, so that I don't have to stop and wash them if I need to switch colors during a project.

Plastic couplers allow you to switch out tips while using the same icing bag. Tip brushes make clean-up a breeze, especially after the tips have been soaked in a glass of warm, soapy water.

Disposable Icing Bags

Promise me you won't try to decorate your cookies with a zip-top bag! Promise? Go with disposable icing bags. These sturdy sacks are up to the task of cookie decorating. If you use them, you won't have to worry about blow-outs or washing out bags between colors.

Measuring Cups and Spoons

You need at least one set of nested measuring cups for dry ingredients and a glass measuring cup for liquids. When measuring flour, always use the spoon and sweep method: Spoon the flour into the cup, mounding it over the top, and then sweep away the excess flour with the flat handle of the spoon. Measuring spoons are a must also. I use two sets when making cookies—one for measuring dry ingredients and one for measuring liquids.

Rolling Pin

I'm partial to my silicone rolling pin, but wood or marble ones work just as well.

Waxed Paper

Rolling cookies on waxed paper helps to prevent sticking and makes for easy clean-up. Waxed paper is also a necessity for tracing images (see page 20).

Parchment Paper

If you've never used parchment paper for baking, you're in for a treat. Give it a try instead of greasing up your cookie sheets. You'll find your cookies won't stick, and they'll brown more evenly. I use parchment paper almost every day

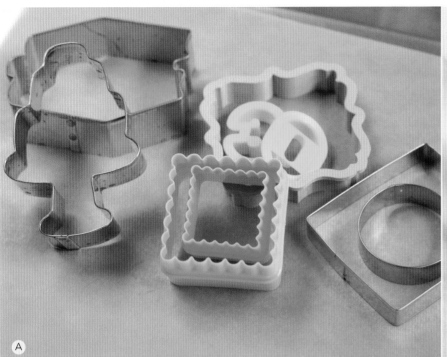

Ⓐ Cookie cutters in an assortment of shapes, sizes, and materials Ⓑ Wood (at right) silicone (middle), and ceramic (at left) rolling pins Ⓒ Nested measuring cups and spoons Ⓓ A disposable icing bag, plastic couplers, and decorating tips Ⓔ Parchment and waxed papers

in my kitchen, not only for cut-out cookies but for lining cake pans and baking scones—you name it. I even use it for roasting Brussels sprouts (hey—we have to balance out those cookies). Because I use parchment for all sorts of baking and cooking, I prefer it to a silicone mat. I never have to worry about getting it sticky or absorbing residual odors from other foods.

You can reuse sheets of parchment. A fresh sheet isn't necessary for every batch of cookies you bake. Look for rolls of parchment near the waxed paper in the grocery store. You can also find pre-cut sheets in kitchen supply stores.

Plastic Wrap
Pressing a piece of plastic wrap onto royal icing will keep it from crusting.

Cookie Sheets
I have lots and lots (and lots!) of cookie sheets, but I only use a select few for baking. I like a sturdy, 11 x 17-inch sheet—it can easily hold six to eight good-sized cookies. I go with nonstick, light-colored sheets. Heavily insulated sheets can leave the bottoms of cookies soft and prone to breakage, while very dark-colored sheets can cause overbrowning.

Since I use cookie sheets to hold cookies for decorating, I have several inexpensive sheets just for this task. When positioning cookies on a sheet, make sure you place them along the edge so that when you rotate the sheet the cookies are always facing you.

Cooling Racks
Wire racks are a must when it's time for cookies to cool.

Cookie Spatula
Specifically made for lifting cookies off a cookie sheet, this thin metal spatula is invaluable.

Silicone Spatulas
Not only are they adorable and available in every color imaginable, silicone spatulas are just the ticket for stirring royal icing and scraping the mixer bowl. Have several sizes on hand.

Sifter
Save your hand muscles and look for the kind with the turn-crank rather than the squeeze handle.

Bowls and Ramekins
It's a good idea to have a variety of these on hand in different sizes. They're helpful for dividing icing into large or small portions based on the cookie design. Ramekins are also perfect for holding sprinkles and add-ons and for mixing luster dust.

Pint Glasses
An easy alternative to the typical icing-bag holder, a pint glass is tall enough and sturdy enough to support several bags without tipping over.

Twist Ties
To prevent drying and overflow, use these to tie off piping bags filled with royal icing.

Squeeze Bottles
Use these instead of unwieldy icing bags when you're working with thinned flood icing. You can find them in the candy-making section of most craft and kitchen supply stores. They come in a variety of sizes, and some have caps that allow you to attach icing tips for filling in small areas. Look for squeeze bottles designed specifically for candy and cookie making. Condiment bottles and those made for other uses may be more difficult to squeeze. Reusing hair-color bottles is not an option!

Toothpicks
Ah, toothpicks...a cookie decorator's best friends. You should have a stash of rounded (not flat) toothpicks for popping air bubbles, guiding icing to edges and corners, and nudging piping that's gone astray. You might even use them to scrape all of the icing off a cookie so that you can start from scratch (I speak from experience).

Dishtowels, Paper Towels, and Aprons
Cookie decorating is a messy business. Keep it clean, people. A damp dishtowel does double duty by keeping flood icing from drying.

Paintbrushes

You'll need paintbrushes for a number of different tasks—painting directly on a cookie, doing brush embroidery, and prepping dried cookies for sanding and sparkling-sugar applications. I have several small-sized brushes, along with medium-sized (think large eyeshadow brush) brushes, flat brushes, and fan brushes. Make sure these brushes are only used in the kitchen.

Tweezers

Keep a fresh set in the kitchen for the precise placement of sprinkles and dragées.

Colored Pencils and Paper

Sketching out a design is always a good idea before putting icing to cookie. Use paper and colored pencils to play with color combinations, tweak patterns, and make notes on which colors you'll need for outlining and flooding.

Basket-Style Coffee Filter

This multitasker can serve as a bowl and as a funnel for applying sprinkles and decorative sugars.

Straws

Paper or plastic, bendy or straight, you'll use straws for poking holes in cookies to make bookmarks, like on page 54, or even ornaments for your Christmas tree!

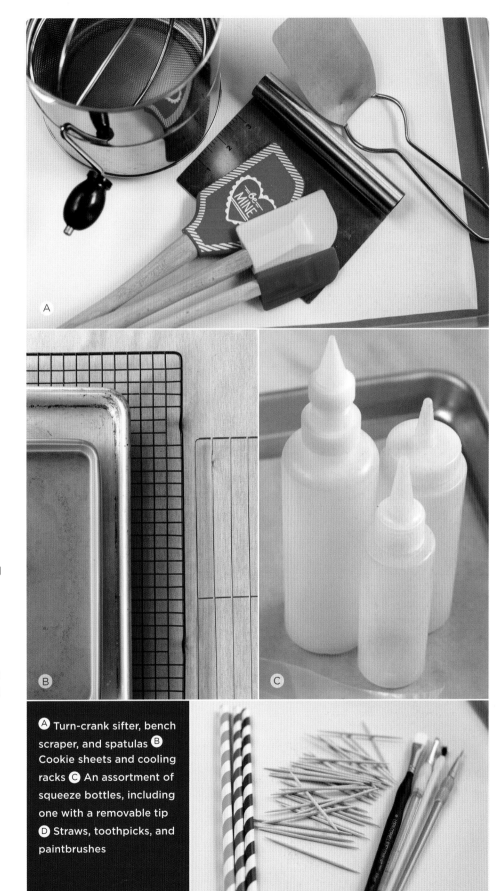

A Turn-crank sifter, bench scraper, and spatulas B Cookie sheets and cooling racks C An assortment of squeeze bottles, including one with a removable tip D Straws, toothpicks, and paintbrushes

Ⓐ From front to back: pastel sprinkles (quins), sugar pearls, and gold dragées Ⓑ Silver and gold luster dust Ⓒ Disco dust: rainbow, gold, and green Ⓓ Food coloring pens and gel paste food coloring

Specialty Ingredients

This is where the fun begins! Gold dragées, multi-colored sprinkles, silver luster dust...your kitchen cabinet will be filled with magic. All of the ingredients you need (the word *need* is used loosely here) can be found at kitchen stores, craft stores, bakery supply shops, and online. For more information, check out the list of resources on page 144.

Meringue Powder

This ingredient is non-negotiable. You'll need it to whip up batches of royal icing. Yes, you can make royal icing with egg whites or egg-white powder; however, I prefer meringue powder because of its stability and because it's easy to work with. (The fact that I don't have to use raw eggs gives me peace of mind!) Different brands of meringue powder vary in taste, so experiment a bit. I prefer the brands that are sold at bakery-supply shops.

Extracts

Look for extracts that are labeled "pure" in order to avoid preservatives and added sugars. If you want your cookies to look really fancy, try vanilla bean paste. It's loaded with real vanilla bean seeds, which will give your cookies lovely flecks of vanilla. For royal icing, you'll want to use a clear extract such as almond to avoid tinting the finished product.

Gel Paste Food Colorings

Another non-negotiable. Unlike liquid food coloring, gel paste food coloring will tint your icing without changing its consistency. A few drops provide a rich, vivid color. I love the gel pastes that come in squeeze bottles. Look for them online and in bakery supply shops.

Note: Yes, there is such a thing as white food coloring, and you'll need it. Royal icing appears to be pure white, but it can turn beige as it dries. Trust me on this one: buy the white food coloring.

Fondant

If you've ever seen a cake with super smooth sides, or sculpted into a shape, chances are it was covered in fondant. Most of the decorated cookies in this book are made with royal icing, but we'll use a bit of fondant now and then. It's fun to branch out! Fondant serves as the base for the Garden Party Cookies on pages 56.

Fondant can be made at home, but I prefer using the store-bought kind most of the time. Different brands of fondant vary greatly in taste, so find one that you like. I recommend trying the brands sold at cake supply and kitchen shops.

Food-Coloring Pens

I always have a set (or two) of these on hand. They're ideal for decorating cookies with kids, and come in handy for adding details such as personalization, and eyes and mouths on faces. Pens with thick tips (great for kids) and thin tips are both available in a range of colors. Always use on icing that is completely dry.

Sanding and Sparkling Sugars

These sugars are probably the easiest way to dress up a cookie. Sanding sugar is a finer grain while sparkling sugar is coarser.

Sprinkles, Jimmies, and Dragées

Oh my! There are many terms and classifications for these tasty embellishments, including *nonpareils* and *quins*. No matter the name, we love them.

Luster Dust

If you've ever seen cookies and cakes colored gold and silver and wondered how that remarkable color was achieved, here's your answer: luster dust. Thinned with an alcohol such as vodka (which evaporates), luster dust is painted on dry icing to create an opaque metallic finish. It can also be brushed on dry to give cookies a beautiful metallic sheen.

Disco Dust

This wonderful dust creates a sparkle like nothing else. Your cookies will twinkle! The full, magical effect is difficult to capture in a photograph, so play Tinkerbell with your cookies and give it a try at home. This product is also sold as fairy dust and pixie dust.

Note: Although metallic add-ons such as luster dust, dragées, and disco dust are labeled nontoxic, the FDA has approved them for decorative use only. That said, did I eat the silver dragées on cupcakes when I was a kid? Yes. Do I eat them now? Yes. Would I eat an entire container of luster dust in one sitting? No. Where these embellishments are concerned, use your best judgment and do what feels right to you.

Getting Started

You're ready now. You have the supplies; your ingredients are on hand. It's time to decorate.

Preparing Your Work Surface

Find a spot with plenty of room to work (I like to stand at my kitchen table when I ice cookies). Put a stepstool or stack of books on the table or counter to elevate your work surface. Place the baked, cooled cookies on cookie sheets so that they line the edges and face out. Avoid putting them in the middle of the sheets—you don't want to reach over cookies while you're decorating. Keep paper towels and toothpicks within reach.

Tinting the Royal Icing

If you've sketched your designs, you know exactly what colors you need. If not, make a list of required colors and whether you'll use them for outlining or flooding. (You'll use more icing while flooding than you will while outlining.) I sometimes cut my notes into strips and place them next to the bowls I plan to use. This is especially helpful when you're using a lot of colors and don't want to end up with a big bowl of purple, when you really only needed a bit.

Divide the icing into bowls and cover them with plastic wrap. Press the wrap directly onto the icing to keep it from crusting. Tint the icing by stirring in small amounts of gel paste coloring until you reach the desired shade. Keep in mind that darker colors such as red, black, and brown will deepen over time, so tint

the icing until it's close to the color you want it to be and then stop. Oversaturated colors can deepen to a shade you didn't want and are also prone to bleeding.

Mixing two different colors is okay and sometimes even necessary to get the precise shade you need. I've learned that mixing more than two colors produces a final shade that isn't especially clear and tends to get muddied.

When tinting shades of the same color (see the Princess Dresses on page 90), start with the lightest shade. Dip a toothpick into the gel paste color and then into the icing. Scoop out some of the lightest shade, and add a bit more coloring for the next darker shade, and so on.

How much coloring should you use? The answer differs for every batch of icing. The amount of coloring you'll need depends on the number of cookies you're decorating, the quantity of icing required in each color, and the particular shade you're tinting. Gel paste colors are very concentrated, so start with just a bit and add more as you need it.

Preparing an Icing Bag

Couplers and tips can seem a little foreign and intimidating if you've never used them before. I promise you'll get the hang of them!

1 Grab a disposable icing bag, insert the large part of the coupler, and slide it all the way down inside the bag. Then use scissors to cut

the bag tip right below the end of the coupler. (The instructions that come with the bags will tell you to cut the tip farther up, near the threads but I find that this leads to leaking bags and no one wants that.) Ⓐ

2 Put a tip on the coupler and secure it with the coupler ring. Ta-da—you just prepared an icing bag! It was easier than you thought, right? Ⓑ

3 Say you want to switch out the tip but continue using the same icing color. No problem. Just twist off the coupler ring, switch the tips, and replace the ring. If you plan to use the first tip again, wrap it in a small piece of plastic wrap to keep the icing from hardening.

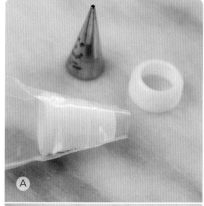

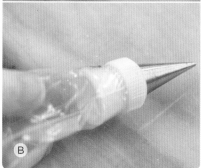

Techniques

Filling an Icing Bag

With the coupler and tip in place, you're ready to fill the icing bag.

1 Open the top of the bag and fold down several inches of it, making a cuff to fit over your non-dominant hand. You can also place the cuffed bag in a pint glass.

2 With your dominant hand, scoop the icing into the bag until it's about half to two-thirds full. Ⓒ

3 Unfold the cuff, bring the bag up, give it a twist, and secure the bag with a twist tie at the top of the icing and at the top of the bag. Ⓓ

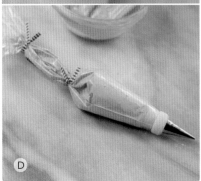

Rolling and Cutting Dough

Forget rolling dough between sheets of waxed paper. Forget using powdered sugar and measuring with wooden dowels. Rolling cookie dough isn't complicated! All you need is flour and a rolling pin.

1 Line your rolling surface with a sheet of waxed paper. This will help prevent sticking and make cleanup easy. Then liberally sprinkle your rolling surface and rolling pin with flour. Ⓔ

2 Grab a portion of dough and knead it with your hands if necessary to make it come together. Using the floured rolling pin, roll the dough out to a thickness of about ¼–⅜ inch. Ⓕ If the dough sticks to the rolling pin, stop and knead it. Roll it around on the floured surface, recoat the rolling pin with flour, and try again.

3 Dip the cookie cutter in flour and then press it into the dough. Repeat, making as many cut-outs in the dough as possible. Ⓖ

4 Remove the scraps of dough that surround the cut-outs. Lift the cut-outs with your hands or a spatula (I tend to do a better job of this when I use my hands) and place them on the prepared cookie sheets. Ⓗ If necessary, recoat your rolling surface and rolling pin with flour. Knead the dough scraps together with the remaining dough and repeat the above steps until all of the dough has been used.

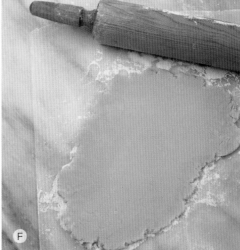

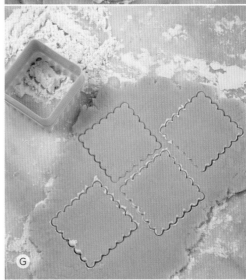

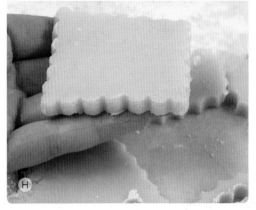

Outlining and Piping

Whether you're outlining a cookie for flooding or adding piping details, you'll use the same technique.

1 Hold the piping bag in your dominant hand at the top of the icing in the bag. Use your other hand to guide the bag along.

2 Squeeze the icing while lifting the bag off of the cookie at an angle as opposed to dragging it on the cookie. Let the icing fall onto the cookie. Ⓛ At the end of the outline, let up on the pressure and lightly touch the tip to the cookie.

The more cookies you decorate, the more confident (and less shaky) you'll be when you outline. Practice on a plate or paper towel before you work on the cookies. If your outline isn't perfect, don't worry. Cookies aren't made to be perfect—they're made to be eaten! You can always nudge your piping into place with a toothpick.

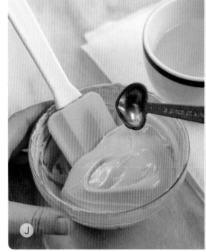

Thinning Icing for Flooding

This may be the most intimidating part of cookie decorating. I promise that after a few batches, you'll get the hang of it. You'll need a bowl of icing, a cup of room-temperature water, some measuring spoons, a silicone spatula, and a damp dishtowel.

1 Add water to the icing by stirring it in slowly with the spatula. This will loosen the icing. The amount of water you use will vary according to the amount of icing you're thinning; I generally start with a teaspoon or two. Keep stirring the water in, gradually decreasing the amount of water you add as you go. Ⓙ

2 Lift the spatula up out of the bowl and drop a ribbon of icing back into the mixture. Ideally, the ribbon should disappear into the remaining icing after a count of "one-thousand-one, one-thousand-two." One-thousand-three is okay,

while four is too thick. Keep testing for consistency and adding water as needed. Toward the end of the process, even a few drops of water will make a difference. Ⓚ

3 To make a slightly thicker flood icing for cookies like the ringed planet on page 84, thin the icing using the same method. Instead of thinning it to a ribbon consistency, run a knife through the center of the icing in the bowl. The line should disappear in 12 to 15 seconds. At that point, the icing is ready.

4 Once the icing has reached the desired consistency, cover it with a damp dishtowel, and let it sit for several minutes. This will give large air bubbles a chance to rise to the surface. Stir the icing gently with a silicone spatula to pop the air bubbles, and then pour it into squeeze bottles for flooding.

Flooding

What does the term "flooding" mean? It's simply a cookie-decorating term for filling a cookie's surface with thinned icing. Squeeze bottles are the best tools for flooding, as thinned icing tends to escape from icing bags.

1 Fill your squeeze bottles with thinned icing and start filling in outlines. Ⓛ I flood cookies three at a time. This gives the icing a chance to spread a bit without setting up. You don't need to be precise here but be sure to flood the cookie pretty generously to avoid thin areas and lumpy, bumpy icing.

2 You'll have some empty spaces, but that's okay—the icing will spread out on its own, and you can help it along with a handy-dandy toothpick. Once you've flooded three cookies, come back to the first one and use a toothpick to coax the icing all the way to the edges and empty places. Ⓜ The icing should be thick enough so that you don't see the cookie underneath. Use a toothpick to pop any large air bubbles.

FLOODING SMALL SPACES

Flooding small spaces, like the numbers on the foam fingers on page 110, can be tricky. Although the task seems easy enough, the icing added to small spaces tends to crater. If this happens, don't worry. To prevent craters, do the following:

Use only as much flood icing as it takes to cover the area. Even though the entire space will be covered after flooding, go ahead and run a toothpick through it. This will dislodge the air bubbles underneath the icing that can cause craters later on. Pesky air bubbles!

NOTE:

→ **Thinning icing with water will not dilute the color.**

→ **Never, ever add water to a squeeze bottle and shake it (unless you want really bubbly icing).**

→ **Adding water is easier than taking it away. If your icing is a little too thin, stir in some sifted powdered sugar to thicken it. The icing will look a little bumpy because of the sugar, but it'll smooth out.**

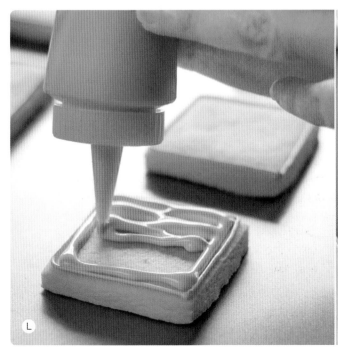

Ⓛ

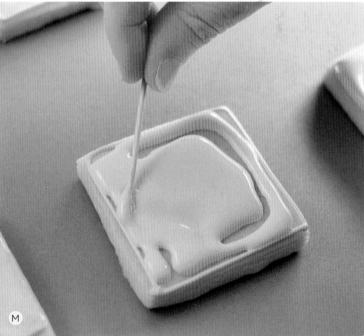

Ⓜ

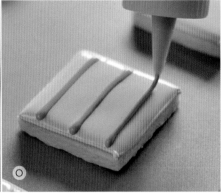

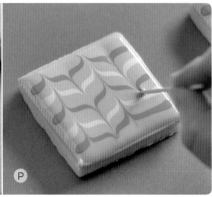

Flood-on-Flood (or Wet-on-Wet)

This decorating technique may be my favorite. If you've ever seen a cookie with flat details (dots, marbling, stripes, hearts) rather than piped details, chances are they were created using this technique. Here's what you do:

1 Thin all of the icing colors you need for your design, making sure each one has the same consistency. Working in batches of six to eight, flood each cookie with the base color. (Working in batches allows the base color to set a bit before adding color on top of it.)

2 Starting with the first cookie you flooded, add contrasting colors on top of the wet base color:

➜ For dots, drop icing straight down onto the base color. Ⓝ

➜ For hearts, drop dots in the same manner but pull a toothpick through the icing to create a heart.

➜ For stripes, drop lines of flood icing on top of the base color. Ⓞ

➜ For marbling, drag a toothpick back and forth across lines or circles. Ⓟ

Applying Add-Ons

I prefer to apply add-ons like sprinkles or sugars to dry, iced cookies. I know this sounds counterintuitive. If sugar will stick to wet icing, why let the icing dry before adding it? The problem is that when you apply add-ons to wet icing, you run the risk of, say, having a stray bit of red sparkling sugar stick in your pristine white icing. Also, it's almost impossible to pick up a wet cookie and shake off excess sprinkles without completely smudging the icing. Here's what I do:

1 Let the cookies dry completely, uncovered, for 6 to 8 hours or overnight.

2 Mix together equal parts meringue powder and water. A good starting amount is ½ teaspoon of each.

3 Use a small, clean paintbrush to apply the mixture to the areas where you want the add-ons to stick.

4 Over a basket-style coffee filter, sprinkle on the add-ons. Shake off the excess into the coffee filter. Use the filter as a funnel to pour the excess back into the container of add-ons. Give the cookies about 30 minutes to set.

For a more precise application, use tweezers to position the add-ons directly onto wet icing (see the eyeglasses on page 47), or use the technique in steps 2 and 3, dotting the meringue powder/water mixture exactly where you'd like the add-ons placed.

Painting

If you're artistically inclined, a solid iced cookie can be your canvas. Even if you're not Picasso, painting on cookies is a lovely way to add detail and interest to a design.

Note: Be sure the base icing is completely dry. Thin the food coloring with an approximately equal amount of water to make your "paint." Dip your paintbrush into the food coloring/water mixture and then blot it well so that you don't saturate the dry icing and ruin the cookie.

Stamping

Talk about an easy way to add interest to a cookie! Stamping is a fairly simple process, but it can get a little messy.

1 Squirt some gel paste food coloring onto an uninked stamp pad or a bed of folded white paper towels. (Use towels that don't have a pressed pattern, as the stamp may not catch the ink in the divots.) You may need to "press" the food coloring into the stamp with a clean paintbrush.

2 Press the stamp into the ink, then test it on a sheet of paper to make sure it's totally saturated. Then press the inked stamp straight down onto the dried royal icing. Press it firmly, but not so hard that you crush the cookie icing. Lift up the stamp, and voilà!

Note: Since the stamp only comes into contact with the cookie for a few seconds, I don't need to worry about it being certified food-safe. However, if this is a concern for you, know that there are food-safe stamps on the market made just for cake and cookie decorating.

Working with Fondant

My medium of choice for cookie decorating is royal icing (page 29), but I love playing with fondant, too. For those unfamiliar with fondant: it's a bit like the modeling compound in the yellow jar that we all played with as kids (but much yummier). You can make it at home, but I typically use store-bought fondant. Look for it in bakery supply shops, craft stores, and online.

Fondant is very easy to work with when you know a few tricks.

1 Coat your rolling surface, rolling pin, and cookie cutter with cornstarch. Don't be afraid of using too much. If you take your fondant from the container and find that it's too hard to manipulate, pop it in the microwave for about 10 seconds on 50% power.

2 When using fondant to cover a cookie, roll it out to a thickness of ⅛–¼ inch. For perfectly even fondant, roll it using dough-rolling sticks. (See resources on page 144.)

3 To adhere fondant to a cookie, apply a light coating of corn syrup to the cookie and place the fondant on top. (See the Garden Party Cookies on page 56 for examples.)

USING MOLDS FOR FONDANT

Silicone molds are a simple way to add dimension and texture to a cookie. They're easy to use.

1 Tint the fondant as needed.

2 Liberally coat the inside of a silicone mold with cornstarch.

3 Roll the fondant into a ball and press it into the mold. Slowly peel the mold back to release the fondant.

4 Use a craft knife to cut away the excess fondant. (The excess can be rerolled and reused.) If cornstarch is visible on the design after unmolding, dab those areas with a damp paintbrush or your finger.

5 Attach the molded shapes to the cookies with a bit of piping consistency royal icing. To add even more dimension to your cookies, use the details from the shape as a guide for applying food coloring "paint" to the design.

Brush Embroidery

An utterly charming way to decorate cookies, brush embroidery looks complicated but is actually quite easy. Cookies decorated using this technique look very elegant and romantic. You'll need cookies that are iced in a solid base color, icing that's of piping consistency, and a damp, flat paintbrush.

1 Starting from the outside and working in, pipe lines for the outer edges to make a flower shape. S

2 Lightly drag the damp paintbrush down toward the center of the flower. Repeat all the way around to make an outer circle of petals. T

3 You can stop here or add more inner layers of petals. For an extra, pretty touch, apply some piping or add-ons to the center of each flower. U

Transferring or Tracing Images

Have you ever seen a cookie that was an absolutely perfect replica of a character or a logo? Or a cookie with printing on it that was so precise it appeared to have been computer-generated? I'll let you in

on a little secret: Those cookies were probably created using an overhead projector designed specifically for cake and cookie decorators who want to recreate images. Doesn't that make you feel better? Me, too!

If you don't have room in your linen closet to store a cookie decorating overhead projector, try this trick—it'll give you similar results:

1 Slide an image under a sheet of waxed paper and trace the image with royal icing. For monograms and simple shapes, icing that's of piping consistency works fine. For logos and the like, use both the outline and flood methods, letting the traced images dry overnight.

2 To apply, simply remove the image from the wax paper and place it on wet icing, or adhere it by "gluing" the image to a cookie with dried icing using a few dabs of royal icing. For an example of adhering dried royal icing embellishments, see page 67.

Note: When adhering an image to wet icing, let the icing settle for 30 minutes or so. This will give any air bubbles a chance to escape before you add the transfer.

Imprinting

Especially useful when you want to pipe a design that's difficult to freehand, imprinting is simply pressing a cookie cutter directly onto cut cookie shapes before, or immediately after, baking. These imprints are then used as templates for piping. For an example, check out the stars on the football helmets. V

Adding Luster Dust Ⓦ

To give your icing a shiny, opaque, metallic finish:

1 In a small bowl or ramekin, mix luster dust with a bit of vodka. Luster dust goes a long way, so start with small amounts, like a ¼ teaspoon, and add several drops of vodka. The mixture should be smooth but not overly thin.

2 Starting with an iced cookie that has completely dried, brush the mixture over the desired area. The alcohol will evaporate, leaving just the metallic finish. Because the alcohol evaporates, you may need to add vodka to the mixture as you're working.

Note: Vodka isn't your only option for applying luster dust, but you should use an alcohol-based substance. You can also use a clear extract, such as lemon. I avoid extracts, though, because they contain oils and can alter the icing's flavor.

The luster dust and vodka mixture can be left to dry at room temperature. The alcohol will evaporate, and the luster dust can be reused. Pretty neat, huh?

For a sheer finish: Simply brush dry luster dust onto a cookie with completely dried icing.

Applying Disco Dust

Ah, disco dust. There's nothing else like it. But be warned: Even with careful application, those sparkly bits end up everywhere. Prepare to find them on your countertops, table, and face!

To apply disco dust, let your cookies dry completely, uncovered, for 6 to 8 hours or overnight. Mix equal parts meringue powder and water together. A good starting amount is ½ teaspoon of each. Use a small, clean paintbrush to apply the mixture wherever you want the disco dust to stick. Over a basket-style coffee filter, sprinkle on the dust. Shake the excess off into the filter. Then use the filter as a funnel to pour the dust back into its original container. Use a clean, dry paintbrush to brush excess dust off of dry areas. You won't get it all, but that's okay. Give the cookies about 30 minutes to set.

Never, ever blow on a disco dust-covered cookie to remove the excess—unless you want to look like a walking disco ball! Not that I've done that myself, of course....

Drying Cookies

Once your cookies are iced, they'll need to dry for 6 to 8 hours or overnight. Let the cookies dry uncovered. Don't worry—they won't go stale. If you're concerned about your dog or cat getting into the cookies, close off the room where they're drying or put a mesh picnic food cover over them.

Royal icing is extremely shiny when it's wet, but it loses most of its shine when it dries. To keep some of the shine, dry the cookies under an oscillating fan or put them in a food dehydrator. If you use a dehydrator, put it on the lowest setting (no higher than 95°) and let it run for a few hours. Then turn it off and let the cookies dry completely.

Making Double-Deckers

As I was dreaming up ideas for cookies for my blog one day, it hit me: Two cookies are better than one! The double-decker cookie was born. Double-deckers consist of a small, decorated cookie that is adhered to a larger one. Once the cookies are decorated and the icing has dried, a small amount of piping-consistency icing is piped onto the back of the smaller cookie and placed onto the front of the larger one. The royal icing acts as a glue of sorts, adhering both, so that you have two cookies in one! For an example, see the double-decker wedding cookies on page 132.

Cookies-on-a-Stick

Want to make a cookie bouquet? Of course you do! First, you'll need cookie sticks, which can be found at craft stores and bakery supply shops. Make sure to buy cookie sticks, not lollipop sticks, which are thinner and won't hold large cookies.

1 Place cookie-dough cut-outs on a cookie sheet, leaving enough room for a cookie stick at the bottom of each. Three will usually fit on one sheet.

2 Bake the cookies as usual. As soon as they come out of the oven, push the cookie sticks up through the bottom of each, about a third to halfway up the cookie. Let the cookies cool on the sheet for five minutes, transfer them to a wire rack, and let them cool completely. The warm dough will adhere to the cookie sticks.

3 Decorate the cookies as usual, taking care not to bump the sticks. If a cookie spins on its stick, remove the stick, squeeze a bit of piping consistency royal icing into the hole, and replace the cookie stick. Let the icing dry for at least 30 minutes.

For mini cookies-on-a-stick (which make cute cupcake toppers), use toothpicks instead of cookie sticks.

Helpful Hints for Cookie Success

Set aside time to decorate. Baking cut-out cookies takes a bit longer than whipping up a batch of chocolate chip cookies, so plan accordingly. I like to bake one day and decorate the next.

Think about supplies before you start. Make sure you have the necessary ingredients and supplies on hand so that you don't have to rush off to the store in the middle of decorating.

Sketch out your designs. It's easier to plan for colors and amounts of icing if you have a strategy for decorating.

Raise your work surface. If you're on the tall side like I am (and even if you're not), your back and shoulders may start to ache after a few hours of bending over a batch of cookies. To remedy this problem, put the cookies on a cookie sheet and set the sheet on a stepstool or stack of cookbooks to raise your work surface.

Practice, practice, practice. Before you begin piping, practice on a plate or paper towel until you're comfortable with the process.

Make extra. This goes for icing and cookies. Always prepare for mess-ups or breakage, which I call lunch.

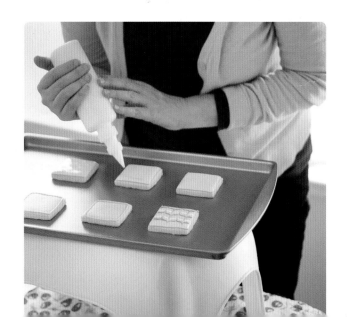

Cookie Care

Storing Cookies

Decorated cookies are tastiest when eaten within a week of baking. Once the icing has dried, store the cookies in individual treat bags or in an airtight container to keep them fresh. Un-iced cookies that have been baked and are completely cool can be stored in an airtight container for a day or two before you decorate them.

Never store decorated cookies in the refrigerator because condensation may ruin the icing.

Freezing

Cookies can be frozen at almost any stage of the process, which makes large projects much more manageable. The dough can be frozen for 3 to 6 months. Simply wrap it in plastic wrap, put it in a freezer bag, and freeze it. You should thaw it at room temperature or in the refrigerator.

My freezer gets a workout because I freeze a lot of baked cookies. When I'm working on a large cookie project, I bake a few dozen when I have time and freeze them. I stack the cookies between layers of waxed paper inside freezer bags and place the bags in hard-sided freezer containers so that they don't get crushed by a stray box of corn dogs. I thaw the cookies at room temperature for a few hours before I decorate them.

Cookies decorated with royal icing can be frozen as well. Make sure the icing is completely dry and follow the instructions for freezing un-iced cookies. I prefer to bag decorated cookies individually for freezing. I thaw them in the packaging at room temperature for several hours—never thaw them in the refrigerator.

Frozen cookies are best consumed within 6 months of freezing. For testing purposes, I kept some in my freezer for over a year, and they were still delicious when I thawed and ate them.

Shipping Cookies

I love to share cookies! Popping a box in the mail for a friend is one of my favorite ways to spread a little sweetness. To ship cookies with minimum (hopefully zero) breakage, here are some tips:

➜ Ship cookies that are simple in shape. Circles, squares, hearts, and other shapes without appendages ship well. Cookies that have delicate appendages—cherries with stems; eight-legged octopuses—don't.

➜ Bag each cookie individually and tie it with a ribbon.

➜ Place the cookies in a sturdy document-style box between layers of bubble wrap or foam sheets. Line the top and bottom of the box with a sheet of foam or bubble-wrap lining. You can fit two layers of cookies in one box.

➜ Close the box and seal it securely with packing tape.

➜ Put the sealed box inside a larger shipping box that's cushioned with packing peanuts.

Note: I like to ship cookies at the beginning of the week so that they don't sit in a warehouse or truck over the weekend.

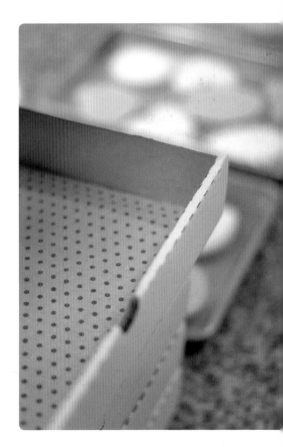

RECITES

Vanilla-Almond Cut-Out Sugar Cookies

Makes 12 to 18 cookies, depending on cookie size

I wish I'd kept count of the number of these cookies I've made over the years. I'd guess it's close to 10,000. Yep, this is my go-to, never-fail recipe. The dough doesn't have to be chilled before it's rolled, and the cookies that result are utterly delicious. Yay!

Note: *I like my sugar cookies thick and on the soft side. If you prefer yours crispy, just roll the dough out a bit thinner.*

YOU WILL NEED

- 3 cups unbleached, all-purpose flour
- 2 teaspoons baking powder
- 1 cup (2 sticks) salted butter, cold and cut into chunks
- 1 cup sugar
- 1 egg
- 3/4 teaspoon pure vanilla extract
- 1/2 teaspoon pure almond extract

■ Position a rack in the center of the oven and preheat the oven to 350°F.

■ Line three cookie sheets with parchment paper.

■ In a medium bowl, whisk together the flour and baking powder. Set this mixture aside.

■ In the large bowl of a stand mixer fitted with a paddle attachment, cream together the butter and sugar until combined and fluffy. Beat in the egg and extracts, mixing until combined.

■ Add the flour mixture in three parts, mixing on low speed. Scrape down the sides and bottoms of the bowl as needed. After the last addition, the dough will look very thick and crumbly.

■ Prepare a rolling surface and roll out a portion of the dough (see Rolling and Cutting Dough on page 15). Cut as many shapes from the dough as possible and place them on a prepared cookie sheet, about 2 inches apart.

Note: If the dough is crumbly or contains bits of unincorporated flour, knead it until it's cohesive and of a uniform consistency.

■ Place the cookie sheet in the freezer for 5 to 10 minutes. Freezing the cookies will help keep them from spreading. Meanwhile, knead the scraps and remaining dough together and continue the rolling, cutting, and freezing process on a second cookie sheet.

■ After freezing, immediately bake the cookies on the center rack of your oven for 9 to 12 minutes (for 3½ to 4-inch cookies), or until they appear done in the center. The baked cookies won't change much in color.

■ Remove the cookies from the oven and let them cool on the cookie sheets for 2 minutes. With a thin cookie spatula, transfer the cookies to a wire rack to cool completely.

Mocha Cut-Out Cookies

Makes 12 to 18 cookies, depending on cookie size

If you're as crazy about the combination of coffee and chocolate as I am, then boy, you're in for a treat. These mocha cookies are dark, rich, and totally irresistible. Try to refrain from eating all of the dough before you bake it—and all of the cookies before you decorate them. Or, go ahead and indulge. I'll never tell.

YOU WILL NEED

- 2½ cups unbleached, all-purpose flour
- ½ cup Dutch-processed cocoa powder
- 2 teaspoons baking powder
- 1 cup (2 sticks) salted butter, cold and cut into chunks
- 1 cup sugar
- 4 teaspoons instant espresso powder
- 1½ teaspoons pure vanilla extract
- 1 egg

▨ Position a rack in the center of the oven and preheat the oven to 350°F.

▨ Line three cookie sheets with parchment paper.

▨ In a medium bowl, whisk together the flour, cocoa, and baking powder. Set this mixture aside.

▨ In the large bowl of a stand mixer fitted with a paddle attachment, cream together the butter and sugar until combined and fluffy.

▨ In a small bowl or ramekin, stir the espresso powder and vanilla together.

▨ Beat in the egg and espresso/vanilla mixture until combined.

▨ Add the flour/cocoa mixture in three parts, mixing on low speed. Scrape down the sides and bottoms of the bowl as needed. After the last addition, the dough will look very thick and crumbly.

▨ The cocoa makes this dough soft and sticky. It'll be easier to work with if you chill it prior to cutting. Divide the dough in half and form it into two discs. Wrap each disc in plastic wrap and refrigerate for 30 minutes before rolling.

▨ Prepare a rolling surface, but instead of coating it with flour alone, cover it with a mixture of cocoa and flour (see Rolling and Cutting Dough on page 15). Roll out one disc of dough. Cut out as many shapes from the dough as possible and place them on a prepared cookie sheet, about 2 inches apart.

Note: If the dough is crumbly or contains bits of unincorporated flour, knead it until it's cohesive and of a uniform consistency.

▨ Place the cookie sheet in the freezer for 5 to 10 minutes. Freezing the cookies will help keep them from spreading. Meanwhile, knead the scraps and remaining dough together and continue the rolling, cutting, and freezing process on a second cookie sheet.

▨ After freezing, immediately place the cookies on the center rack of your oven and bake them for 9 to 12 minutes (for 3½ to 4-inch cookies) or until they appear done in the center. The baked cookies won't change much in color.

▨ Remove the cookies from the oven and let them cool on the cookie sheets for 2 minutes. With a thin cookie spatula, transfer the cookies to a wire rack to cool completely.

Note: Look for Dutch-processed cocoa powder and instant espresso powder in your local grocery store. The cocoa can be found on the baking aisle. The espresso powder will be located in the coffee section. Both are available online.

Brown Sugar and Spice Cookies

Makes 12 to 18 cookies, depending on cookie size

These cookies are a bit softer than typical cut-outs because of the brown sugar. The light spices make them a great alternative to ginger-bread. Perfect if you're craving a little taste of Christmas in the middle of July.

YOU WILL NEED

- 3 cups unbleached, all-purpose flour
- 2 teaspoons baking powder
- ½ teaspoon cinnamon
- ¼ teaspoon ginger
- ⅛ teaspoon freshly grated nutmeg
- ⅛ teaspoon allspice
- ⅛ teaspoon cloves
- 1 cup (2 sticks) salted butter, cold and cut into chunks
- 1 cup light-brown sugar (packed)
- 1 egg
- 1 teaspoon pure vanilla extract

▨ Position a rack in the center of the oven and preheat the oven to 350°F.

▨ Line three cookie sheets with parchment paper.

▨ In a medium bowl, whisk together the flour, baking powder, and spices. Set this mixture aside.

▨ In the large bowl of a stand mixer fitted with a paddle attachment, cream together the butter and brown sugar until combined and fluffy. Beat in the egg and vanilla, mixing until combined.

▨ Add the flour mixture in three parts, mixing on low speed. Scrape down the sides and bottom of the bowl as needed. After the last addition, the dough will look very thick and crumbly.

▨ Prepare a rolling surface and roll out a portion of the dough (see Rolling and Cutting Dough on page 15). Cut as many shapes from the dough as possible and place them on a prepared cookie sheet, about 2 inches apart.

Note: If the dough is crumbly or contains bits of unincorporated flour, knead it together until it's cohesive and of a uniform consistency.

▨ Place the cookie sheet in the freezer for 5 to 10 minutes. Freezing the cookies will help keep them from spreading. Meanwhile, knead the scraps and remaining dough together and continue the rolling, cutting, and freezing process on a second cookie sheet.

▨ After freezing, immediately place the cookies on the center rack of your oven and bake them for 9 to 12 minutes (for 3½ to 4-inch cookies) or until they appear done in the center. The baked cookies won't change much in color.

▨ Remove the cookies from the oven and let them cool on the cookie sheets for 2 minutes. With a thin cookie spatula, transfer the cookies to a wire rack to cool completely.

Pink Lemonade Cookies

Makes 12 to 18 cookies, depending on cookie size

Love a little tart with your sweet? Then these cookies are for you. They're tangy, sharp, and PINK! Amp up the tartness even more by adding ¼ teaspoon of pure lemon extract to your royal icing.

YOU WILL NEED

- 3 cups unbleached, all-purpose flour
- 2 teaspoons baking powder
- 1 cup (2 sticks) salted butter, cold and cut into chunks
- ½ cup sugar
- ½ cup thawed pink lemonade concentrate
- 1 egg
- pink gel paste food coloring (optional)

Note: The pink lemonade concentrate is very pink, but the egg will give it a yellowish tinge, and the flour will make it less bright. For a vibrant pink, add the pink gel paste food coloring.

▓ In a medium bowl, whisk together the flour and the baking powder. Set this mixture aside.

▓ In the large bowl of a stand mixer fitted with a paddle attachment, cream together the butter and sugar until combined and fluffy. Beat in the lemonade concentrate. (The mixture will look a little like pink cottage cheese, but that's okay.) Add the egg and food coloring, mixing until combined.

▓ Add the flour mixture in three parts, mixing on low speed. Scrape down the sides and bottom of the bowl as needed. The dough will be quite sticky. (If the dough isn't as pink as you'd like it to be, knead in more food coloring before rolling.)

▓ Wrap the dough in plastic wrap and refrigerate it for at least one hour before rolling.

▓ Position a rack in the center of the oven and preheat the oven to 350°F.

▓ Line three cookie sheets with parchment paper.

▓ Prepare a rolling surface and roll out a portion of the dough (see Rolling and Cutting Dough on page 15). Cut as many shapes from the dough as possible and place them on a prepared cookie sheet, about 2 inches apart.

▓ Place the cookie sheet in the freezer for 5 to 10 minutes. Freezing the cookies will help keep them from spreading. Meanwhile, knead the scraps and remaining dough together and continue the rolling, cutting, and freezing process on a second cookie sheet.

▓ After freezing, immediately place the cookies on the center rack of your oven and bake them for 9 to 12 minutes (for 3½ to 4-inch cookies) or until they appear done in the center. The baked cookies won't change much in color.

▓ Remove the cookies from the oven and let them cool on the cookie sheets for 2 minutes. With a thin cookie spatula, transfer the cookies to a wire rack to cool completely.

Gluten-Free Chocolate Cut-Out Cookies

Makes 12 to 18 cookies, depending on cookie size

A large part of my world revolves around all-purpose flour. I know though, that many of you can't eat wheat flour. I also know that you need cookies. These chocolate cookies have a lovely, mild, milk-chocolatey taste that are a big hit with kids!

Note: Oat flour is naturally gluten free but is sometimes processed with wheat ingredients. Look for oat flour that's specifically labeled "gluten free."

If gluten-free isn't a concern for you, replace the oat flour, potato flour, and cornstarch with 2⅔ cups unbleached, all-purpose flour. Omit the xanthan gum, and add 2 teaspoons baking powder.

YOU WILL NEED

- ⅓ cup Dutch-processed cocoa powder
- 1⅔ cups gluten-free oat flour
- ⅔ cup finely ground potato flour
- ⅓ cup cornstarch
- 1 teaspoon xanthan gum
- 1 cup (2 sticks) salted butter, cold and cut into chunks
- 1 cup sugar
- 1 egg
- 1½ teaspoons pure vanilla extract (gluten free)

■ In a medium bowl, whisk together the cocoa powder, oat flour, potato flour, cornstarch, and xanthan gum. Set this mixture aside.

■ In the large bowl of a stand mixer fitted with a paddle attachment, cream together the butter and sugar until combined and fluffy. Beat in the egg and vanilla, mixing until combined.

■ Add the oat flour mixture in three parts, mixing on low speed. Scrape down the sides and bottom of the bowl as needed.

■ Wrap the dough in plastic wrap and refrigerate it for at least one hour before rolling.

■ Position a rack in the center of the oven and preheat the oven to 350°F.

■ Line three cookie sheets with parchment paper.

■ Prepare a rolling surface, coating it with a mixture of oat flour and cocoa powder (see Rolling and Cutting Dough on page 15). Roll out a portion of the dough. Cut as many shapes as possible from dough and place them on a prepared cookie sheet, about 2 inches apart.

■ Place the cookie sheet in the freezer for 5 to 10 minutes. Freezing the cookies will help keep them from spreading. Meanwhile, knead the scraps and remaining dough together and continue the rolling, cutting, and freezing process on a second cookie sheet.

■ After freezing, immediately place the cookies on the center rack of your oven and bake them for 9 to 12 minutes (for 3½ to 4-inch cookies) or until they appear done in the center.

■ Remove the cookies from the oven and let them cool on the cookie sheets for 2 minutes. With a thin cookie spatula, transfer the cookies to a wire rack to cool completely.

Royal Icing

Makes enough to cover 3 to 6 dozen 4-inch cookies, depending on the number of colors and amount of detail involved

Why use royal icing? It's the ideal medium for decorating cookies. It dries hard and opaque, and cookies iced with it are stackable and easy to package and ship. Also, cookies decorated with royal icing can be stored at room temperature or frozen (yes, frozen!).

Feel free to halve this recipe if you're only making a dozen or so cookies. I like to start with plenty of icing so that I don't have to stop in the middle of decorating to make more.

You'll use this recipe for both piping and flooding—or filling in—cookies (see Thinning Icing for Flooding on page 16).

YOU WILL NEED

- ½ cup meringue powder
- 1 scant cup water (meaning just a little less than 1 cup)
- 2 pounds (32 ounces) powdered sugar
- 2 teaspoons light corn syrup
- ½ teaspoon clear extract, optional (see note)

Note: Feel free to add an extract to your royal icing, but stick to clear extracts such as almond or lemon to avoid tinting the icing. I always use almond with the vanilla-almond cut-outs.

■ In the large bowl of a stand mixer fitted with a paddle attachment, mix together the meringue powder and water until the mixture is foamy and no lumps remain. Scrape down the sides of the bowl as needed.

■ Sift in the powdered sugar, add the corn syrup and extract (if using), and beat on low until the powdered sugar is incorporated. Scrape down the sides and bottom of the bowl.

■ Increase the mixer's speed to medium-low and beat for 5 minutes. Ⓐ

■ Increase the mixer's speed to medium-high and continue beating just until the icing is glossy and holds a stiff peak. During the mixing process, it's okay to stop and check the status of the icing every so often to avoid overbeating. To check for stiff peaks, remove the beater from the mixer and hold it so that the icing is pointing up in the air. If the peak is floppy, keep beating. If the icing holds a point when jiggled, it's ready. Ⓑ

■ Immediately divide the icing into bowls. Press plastic wrap down onto the icing to keep it from crusting. It's now ready for tinting. Ⓒ

A

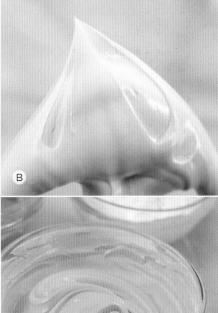

B

C

Troubleshooting

The cookie dough is crumbly.
After mixing, try kneading the dough, especially the crumbly bits at the bottom of the bowl.

The cookies spread while baking.
Freezing cut-out shapes for 5 to 10 minutes prior to baking will help prevent spreading. Also, never place cut-outs you're planning to bake on a warm cookie sheet.

The royal icing is tacky and/or pitted after drying.
This happens when the flood icing is too thin. If you suspect you've thinned your icing a bit too much, stir in some sifted powdered sugar until it reaches the "one-thousand-one, one-thousand-two" stage described on page 16.

The cookies dried with dark splotches.
This is most likely due to humidity. Try drying your cookies someplace besides the kitchen, where water and steam from the stove add moisture to the air. (I dry my cookies on the dining room table.) If it's hot and humid outside, be sure to run the air conditioner in your house. Also, keep the windows closed while your cookies are drying.

The cookies dried with white splotches.
A stray drop of water in your flood icing can result in white splotches that appear while the icing dries. Check your squeeze bottles for water drops before you fill them. Wipe all water from the sides of mixing bowls before pouring their contents into bottles. If you notice a drop of water while you're icing, blot it with a paper towel and then add more flood icing.

The royal icing is full of bubbles.
Two hints here...ONE: Gently stir in the water for flooding with a rubber spatula; don't use a mixer. TWO: Once the water is incorporated, cover the icing with a damp dishtowel and let it sit for several minutes. Most of the bubbles will rise to the surface. Stir the icing gently one more time, and you should be good to go. Any other stray bubbles can be popped with a toothpick or a pin.

Do not ever, EVER add water to a squeeze bottle of icing and shake it.

The icing flakes once it's dried.
Overbeaten icing can be dry, brittle, and flaky. When you make royal icing, beat it until the icing comes to a peak and stop. Also, be sure to use a paddle attachment when beating.

The icing is stiff and breaks during piping.
The icing may have been overbeaten or need a little more water. Squeeze the icing back into a bowl and gently stir in a few drops of water to loosen it.

My hands cramp while I'm piping.
Try filling your icing bags until they're only half or two-thirds full. This will ease cramps.

Icing Storage

Royal icing can be made and refrigerated several days ahead of time, but keep in mind that it will loosen as time goes by. For intricate piping work, lettering, or small details, use the icing on the day it's made. If you're using icing that's been refrigerated, let it come to room temperature and then stir it to incorporate any liquid that may have collected on the bottom of the bowl. If the icing seems too loose to work with, stir in some sifted powdered sugar to thicken it up.

Royal icing can dry out very quickly, so keep it covered with a piece of plastic wrap. Place the wrap directly on top of the icing.

Thinned icing should be used the same day you make it. It'll separate over time, so if you're working with the same bottle over the course of several hours, stir it occasionally by gently swirling a chopstick or table knife around in the bottle. Don't ever shake thinned icing in a squeeze bottle. You'll be left with millions of tiny air bubbles.

I'm having trouble with red and black icings.

These icings are the hardest to work with. Both can have terrible aftertastes, and getting the right depth of color for each can be difficult. Look for gel paste food colorings labeled as "super" red and black. These will give you the deep, rich colors you're looking for, and you won't have to use up the jars of paste trying to achieve them. Plus, there's no awful aftertaste.

The icing dries with craters.

See the tips for flooding small areas on page 17.

The icing tips clog.

Mixing the meringue powder with water and using sifted powdered sugar while you make the royal icing should prevent this. If a tip continues to clog, remove it and press the clog through with a toothpick.

The piped icing spreads.

When icing sits for a while or is stored, it loses its stiffness. To remedy this problem, stir in sifted powdered sugar until the icing thickens. Sugar granules may appear in the icing during this process. Don't worry—they'll disappear.

The icing bleeds.

Every cookie maker faces this problem at some point. Don't panic! To prevent bleeding, use a high-quality gel paste food coloring. You only need to use a bit of gel paste to achieve the deep hues you're looking for. Also, take care not to over-saturate the icing; colors (especially dark ones) will deepen over time. If you're creating a flood-on-flood design, give the base color several minutes to set before adding the detail colors. If you're filling in a dark outline with a lighter color, let the outline set for at least an hour before flooding it.

An assortment of cookies decorated by guests at the Hubbell & Hudson Viking Cooking School cookie party (see page 33 for more photos).

Cookie Party!

A cookie can be more than the star of the dessert table—it can be a celebration in itself! A cookie decorating party is a fun idea for birthdays, holidays, and just about any other occasion that calls for some special merrymaking. With a little planning, a cookie party is a cinch to pull off.

Hosting a Cookie Party for Adults:

A FEW MONTHS BEFORE THE BIG EVENT:

➜ Bake and freeze cut-out cookies
➜ Order supplies such as icing bags, squeeze bottles, couplers, tips, boxes, sugars, and sprinkles.
A day or two before the party:
➜ Make and tint the royal icing and store it in the refrigerator.
➜ Thaw the cookies at room temperature.

DAY OF THE PARTY:

➜ An hour or two prior to the arrival of your guests, transfer some of the icing to piping bags, secure the tops with twist ties, and place them in pint glasses.
➜ Thin the remaining icing for flooding and pour it into squeeze bottles.
➜ Place sprinkles and sugars in small bowls and ramekins.
➜ Give each guest a cookie sheet or tray, toothpicks, and a paper towel.
➜ Let the guests go to town, outlining and flooding cookies.
➜ The icing will be wet, so provide guests with flat boxes for transporting their cookies home. Pizza boxes work well.

OPTIONAL:

➜ Decorate a few examples showing different techniques, such as dots and marbling.
➜ Ask each guest to bring un-iced cookies for decorating.
➜ Serve snacks such as cheese, crackers, and fruit to counterbalance the sugar (wine is good, too).
➜ Provide aprons, or ask each guest to bring one.
➜ Award prizes for prettiest, silliest, and most colorful cookies.
➜ Print the cookie and icing recipes onto recipes cards for each guest to take home.
➜ Make theme cookies like the ones shown in this book.

Cookie Decorating Party with Kids:

Let's be totally honest here: decorating cookies with the kiddos probably isn't going to be anything like the commercials you see on TV—the ones in which the kitchen is sparkling clean, the cookies are works of art, and everyone is smiling. In the real world, sprinkles are going to get scattered across the floor, fingers will poke through icing, and a few tears may be shed (by the kids, too).

So, keep in mind that decorating cookies with little ones will be messy, and that children have very short attention spans. It's a process that probably won't go perfectly, like that TV commercial. Also, strike this sentence from your vocabulary, "Here, let me help you with that."

Here are a few tips for creating pleasant cookie-decorating memories with kids:

➜ Remember that the outlining of designs is difficult for kids. Use the thicker-consistency flood icing (details on page 16) in squeeze bottles. Don't use icing bags.
➜ Have everything ready—cookies baked, icing tinted, sprinkles and supplies set out—before you call the kids into the kitchen.
➜ Give each child a cookie sheet or rimmed paper plate for catching loose sprinkles while decorating.
➜ If you're at home, have the kids wash their hands before they start. If you're decorating with a class or group of kids, have hand sanitizer at the ready.
➜ If you're going to be working with a group of kids, place the sprinkles and sugars in small bowls with disposable spoons rather than setting out the full jars. You don't want an entire jar of sprinkles dumped onto a single cookie. It can happen—I've seen it!
➜ If you're making cookies to save for later, make sure you have a cookie for each child to eat while at the party.
➜ If the idea of kids running loose with icing scares you, plan a cookie party that features interacting with the cookies, rather than decorating, like the monster cookies featured on pages 68. Alternatively, bake the cookies, ice them in white, and let the kiddos go wild with food-coloring pens.

How to Host a Cookie Exchange

A party that concludes with each guest going home with dozens of homemade cookies is my kind of party! Hosting one is a snap.

ONE MONTH AHEAD:

➜ Send out invitations, asking each guest to RSVP and state which type of cookie they'd like to bring. (This will help to avoid all guests bringing the same variety of cookie.)

➜ Once the RSVP count is in, contact guests with the amount of cookies they'll need to bring. Typically, you'll want each guest to bring 1 dozen for each party guest, plus an extra dozen for sampling. (For example, if six people are attending, each guest will bring 7 dozen cookies.) Feel free to scale down to ½ dozen per person.

➜ Ask each guest to either print their recipe for each person to take home, or email the recipe to you, the host, to print out for each guest. Cute recipe cards are a special touch.

FOR THE PARTY:

➜ On a large table, or a few small ones, set out platters for each cookie variety. Placecards are helpful for identifying varieties. Set the printed recipes next to each platter.

➜ Provide snacks, coffee, tea, and a large platter for holding the cookies for sampling.

➜ Give each guest a large bakery box or container, or ask them to bring their own, for packaging. Each guest will take home 1 dozen of each variety of cookie. Waxed paper, cello bags, twine, ribbon, and labels let your guests get creative with the packaging.

Cookie decorating party at the Hubbell & Hudson Viking Cooking School, The Woodlands, Texas

BIRTHDAY PARTY

Everybody knows that birthdays call for an extra-special dessert! Bake up a batch of these sweet treats for a special celebration or mail them off to the birthday girl (or boy)!

NUMBERS

you will need

Vanilla-Almond Sugar Cookies
(page 24), numbers

Royal icing (page 29) tinted: GREEN

Disposable icing bag

Coupler

Icing tip: #2

Squeeze bottle

Toothpicks

Meringue powder

Small paintbrush

Green disco dust

1 Scoop some green icing into a bag fitted with a #2 tip,
and outline the numbers. (A)

2 Thin the green icing for flooding (see page 16). Cover
it with a damp dishtowel and let it sit for several minutes.
Gently stir it with a silicone spatula and transfer it to a
squeeze bottle.
→ Fill in the outlined areas with the thinned icing. Use a toothpick to guide the icing to the edges and pop air bubbles. (B)
→ Let the cookies dry uncovered for 6 to 8 hours or overnight.

3 When the cookies are dry, apply green disco dust:
Mix ¼ teaspoon meringue powder with ¼ teaspoon water.
Use a small paintbrush to apply the mixture to the cookies.
Sprinkle on the disco dust and shake off the excess (see page 21
for details on applying disco dust).

Note: Instead of disco dust, feel free to use sanding sugar.

A

B

BIRTHDAY PARTY

PRESENTS

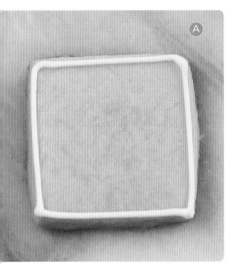

you will need

Vanilla-Almond Sugar Cookies (page 24), square

Royal icing (page 29), divided and tinted:
WHITE • YELLOW • BLUE • PINK

Disposable icing bags (4)

Couplers

Icing tips: #2, #1

Squeeze bottle

Toothpicks

Multi-colored sprinkles

Fondant, tinted green

Silicone bow mold

Green gel paste food coloring

Small paintbrush

1 Scoop some white icing into a bag fitted with a #2 tip, and outline the cookie. Ⓐ

2 Thin the white icing for flooding (see page 16). Cover it with a damp dishtowel and let it sit for several minutes. Gently stir it with a silicone spatula and transfer it to a squeeze bottle.
→ Fill in the outlined areas with the thinned icing. Use a toothpick to guide the icing to the edges and pop air bubbles.
→ Scatter sprinkles across the wet icing. Ⓑ
→ Let the cookies dry for at least one hour.

3 Use #1 tips to pipe streamers onto the cookie in yellow, pink, or blue. Ⓒ
→ Let the cookies dry uncovered for 6 to 8 hours or overnight.

4 Press the green fondant into the prepared silicone bow mold (see page 19). Trim off the excess.

5 Pipe a small amount of piping-consistency icing onto the back of a bow and lightly press it on top of one of the present cookies.

6 Mix one drop of water with one drop of green gel paste food coloring. Dip a small paintbrush into the mixture, dab the excess off on a paper towel, and apply the gel paste "paint" to the bow.
→ Allow 30 minutes for the bows to adhere to the cookies before you stack or package the batch.

HAPPY BIRTHDAY GARLAND

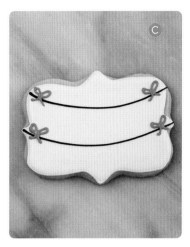

you will need

Vanilla-Almond Sugar Cookies (page 24), scalloped plaque shape

Royal icing (page 29), divided and tinted:
WHITE • BLACK • GREEN • BLUE • PINK • YELLOW • ORANGE

Disposable icing bags (7)

Couplers

Icing tips: #2, #1

Squeeze bottle

Toothpicks

1 Scoop some white icing into a bag fitted with a #2 tip, and outline the cookie. Ⓐ

2 Thin the white icing for flooding (see page 16). Cover it with a damp dishtowel and let it sit for several minutes. Gently stir it with a silicone spatula and transfer it to a squeeze bottle.
→ Fill in the outlined areas with the thinned icing. Use a toothpick to guide the icing to the edges and pop air bubbles. Ⓑ
→ Let the cookies dry for at least one hour.

3 Pipe on the following details:
→ Use a #1 tip with black icing to add two curved lines across each cookie.
→ Use a #1 tip with green icing to make bows at each end of the strings. Ⓒ

4 Use a #1 tip with green, blue, pink, yellow, and orange icing to make letters for the garland. Ⓓ
→ Let the cookies dry uncovered for 6 to 8 hours or overnight.

Tip: The easiest way to center printed words across a cookie is to start with the middle letters and work your way out to each end.

CAKES ON PEDESTALS

 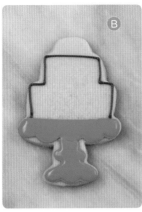   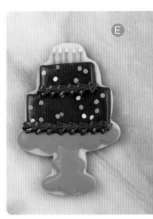

you will need

Vanilla-Almond Sugar
Cookies (page 24), cake
on pedestal shape

Royal icing (page 29),
divided and tinted:
GREEN • CHOCOLATE BROWN •
BLUE • YELLOW

Disposable icing bags (4)

Couplers

Icing tips: #2, #1, star tip

Squeeze bottles (2)

Toothpicks

Multi-colored sprinkles

Rainbow disco dust

Meringue powder

Small paintbrush

1 Scoop some green icing into a bag fitted with a #2 tip, and outline the pedestal. Ⓐ

→ Thin the green icing for flooding (see page 16). Cover it with a damp dishtowel and let it sit for several minutes. Gently stir it with a silicone spatula and transfer it to a squeeze bottle.

2 Fill in the outlined area with the thinned green icing. Use a toothpick to guide the icing to the edges and pop air bubbles.

3 Scoop some brown icing into a bag, attach a #2 tip, and outline the shape of the cake. Reserve some of the brown icing in the bag for piping details later. Ⓑ

4 Thin the brown icing for flooding (see page 16). Cover it with a damp dishtowel and let it sit for several minutes. Gently stir it with a silicone spatula and transfer it to a squeeze bottle.

→ Fill in the outlined area with the thinned brown icing. Use a toothpick to guide the icing to the edges and pop air bubbles.

→ Scatter the sprinkles over the wet brown icing. Ⓒ

→ Let the cookies dry for at least one hour.

5 Pipe on the following details:

→ Use #1 tips with green and blue icing to add candles

→ Use a #1 tip with yellow icing to add flames to the candles Ⓓ

6 Use a star tip with brown icing to pipe a ruffle border across the bottom of each cake layer. Ⓔ

→ Let the cookies dry uncovered for 6 to 8 hours or overnight.

7 When the cookies are dry, apply rainbow disco dust to the candle flames: Mix ¼ teaspoon meringue powder with ¼ teaspoon water. Use a small paintbrush to apply the mixture to the flame. Sprinkle on the disco dust and shake off the excess (see page 21 for details on applying disco dust).

CAKE SLICES

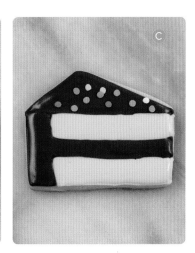

you will need

Vanilla-Almond Sugar Cookies (page 24), cake slice shape

Royal icing (page 29), divided and tinted:
CHOCOLATE BROWN • YELLOW

Disposable icing bags (2)

Couplers

Icing tips: #2, star tip

Squeeze bottles (2)

Toothpicks

Multi-colored sprinkles

1 Scoop some brown icing into a bag fitted with a #2 tip, and outline the top, middle, and outer edge of the cake slice. A Reserve some of the brown icing in the bag for adding piping details later.

2 Scoop some yellow icing into a bag, attach a #2 tip, and outline the remainder of the cake.

3 Thin the brown and yellow icings for flooding (see page 16). Cover them with a damp dishtowel and let them sit for several minutes. Gently stir them with a silicone spatula and transfer them to squeeze bottles as needed.
→ Fill in the brown outlines with the thinned brown icing. Use a toothpick to guide the icing to the edges and pop air bubbles.
→ Scatter the sprinkles over the wet brown icing. B

4 Fill in the yellow outlines with the thinned yellow icing. Use a toothpick to guide the icing to the edges and pop air bubbles. C
→ Let the cookies dry for at least one hour.

5 Use a star tip with the brown icing to pipe a ruffle border across the top edge of the cookie. D
→ Let the cookies dry uncovered for 6 to 8 hours or overnight.

CANDLES

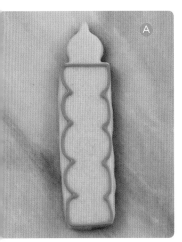 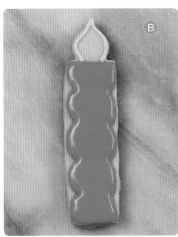 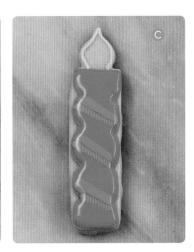 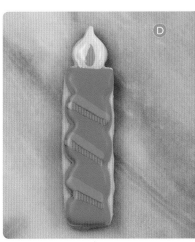

you will need

Vanilla-Almond Sugar Cookies
(page 24), candle shape

Royal icing (page 29), divided and
tinted:
GREEN • YELLOW • BLUE •
PINK • ORANGE

Disposable icing bags (2)

Couplers

Icing tip: #2

Squeeze bottles (5)

Toothpicks

Rainbow disco dust

Small paintbrush

Meringue powder

1 Scoop some green icing into a bag fitted with a #2 tip, and outline the base of the candle. Ⓐ

2 Scoop some yellow icing into a bag fitted with a #2 tip, and outline the candle flame.

3 Thin the green, blue, pink, yellow, and orange icings for flooding (see page 16). Cover them with a damp dishtowel and let them sit for several minutes. Gently stir them with a silicone spatula and transfer them to squeeze bottles as needed.
→ Working 6 to 8 cookies at a time, fill in the outlined areas with the thinned green icing. Use a toothpick to guide the icing to the edges and pop air bubbles. Ⓑ

4 Beginning with the first cookie you flooded, add lines of blue and pink on top of the wet green icing. Ⓒ

5 Using the same method, fill in the candle flames with yellow icing and add thinned orange icing on top. Ⓓ
→ Let the cookies dry uncovered for 6 to 8 hours or overnight.

6 When the cookies are dry, apply rainbow disco dust to the candle flames: Mix ¼ teaspoon meringue powder with ¼ teaspoon water. Use a small paintbrush to apply the mixture to the flame. Sprinkle on the disco dust and shake off the excess (see page 21 for details on applying disco dust).

BOOK CLUB

I've never been in a book club,
but from what I understand,
food is essential! And wine,
too, of course...
Note: Add a bit of ivory icing
to your cookies to give them
an antique look.

EYEGLASSES

you will need

Mocha Cut-Out Cookies
(page 25), eyeglasses shape
(template, page 143)

Royal icing (page 29),
divided and tinted:
**FOREST GREEN (MEDIUM
SHADE)** • **IVORY**

Disposable icing bags (2)

Couplers

Icing tips: #2, #1

Squeeze bottles (2)

Toothpicks

Tweezers

Gold dragées

1 Scoop some medium green icing into a bag fitted with a #2 tip. Outline
the glasses and pipe the edges of the lenses. Ⓐ

2 Thin the green and ivory icings for flooding (see page 16). Cover them
with a damp dishtowel and let them sit for several minutes. Gently stir
them with a silicone spatula and transfer them to squeeze bottles as needed.
→ Fill in the outlined areas with the thinned icing. Use a toothpick to guide
the icing to the edges and pop air bubbles. Ⓑ

3 While the green icing is still wet, use tweezers to place gold dragées
in the corners of the eyeglasses.

4 Use a #1 tip with ivory icing to pipe details on the lenses. Ⓒ
→ Let the cookies dry uncovered for 6 to 8 hours or overnight.

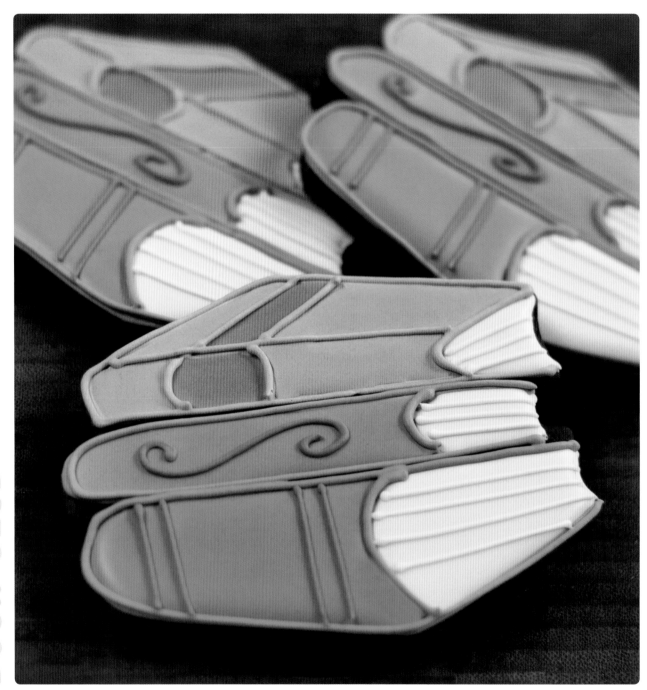

STACKS OF BOOKS

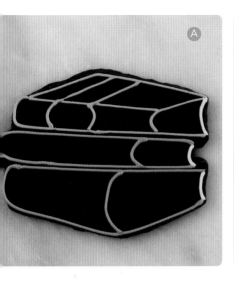

you will need

Mocha Cut-Out Cookies (page 25), book stack shape

Royal icing (page 29), divided and tinted:

BURGUNDY (MEDIUM AND DARK SHADES) • BLUE (MEDIUM AND DARK SHADES) • FOREST GREEN (MEDIUM AND DARK SHADES) • IVORY

Disposable icing bags (6)

Couplers

Icing tips: #2, #1

Squeeze bottles (5)

Toothpicks

1 Scoop some of the lighter shades of burgundy, blue, and green icings into bags fitted with #2 tips. Outline each of the books with the icings. Section off a portion of the burgundy book for filling in with the darker shade of burgundy icing.

2 Scoop some of the ivory icing into a bag, attach a #2 tip, and outline the book's pages. A
→ Reserve some of each icing in the bags for piping details later.

3 Thin the medium burgundy, dark burgundy, medium blue, medium green, and ivory icings for flooding (see page 16). Cover them with a damp dishtowel and let them sit for several minutes. Gently stir them with a silicone spatula and transfer them to squeeze bottles as needed.
→ Fill in the outlined areas with the thinned icing. Use a toothpick to guide the icing to the edges and pop air bubbles. B

4 Pipe on the following details:
→ Use a #2 tip and the lighter burgundy, blue, and green icings to pipe over the outlines of the books.
→ Use #1 tips with dark blue and dark green icing to add detail piping. C
→ Use a #1 tip with ivory icing to pipe lines for the pages.
→ Let the cookies dry uncovered for 6 to 8 hours or overnight.

WINE BOTTLES

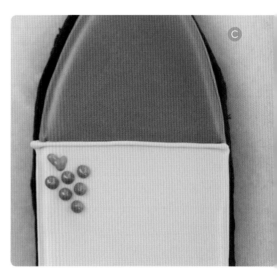

you will need

Mocha Cut-Out Cookies (page 25), wine bottle shape

Royal icing (page 29), divided and tinted:
BURGUNDY • FOREST GREEN • IVORY

Disposable icing bags (3)

Couplers

Icing tips: #2, #1

Squeeze bottles (3)

Toothpicks

Black food-coloring pen

1 Scoop some of the burgundy, green, and ivory icings into bags fitted with #2 tips. Outline each of the bottles, using ivory for the label, burgundy for the bottle, and green for the top. Reserve some of each piping-consistency icing for adding details later. Ⓐ

2 Thin the icings for flooding (see page 16). Cover them with a damp dishtowel and let them sit for several minutes. Gently stir them with a silicone spatula and transfer them to squeeze bottles as needed.
→ Fill in the outlined areas with the thinned icing. Use a toothpick to guide the icing to the edges and pop air bubbles. Ⓑ

3 Use #1 tips to pipe over the outline of the top in green icing, and the top and bottom of the label with ivory icing.

4 Pipe dots onto the label with burgundy icing to form a cluster of grapes using a #1 tip. Use a #1 to add a stem to the grapes. Ⓒ
→ Let the cookies dry uncovered for 6 to 8 hours or overnight.

5 Once the cookies are completely dry, use a black food coloring marker to write the name of the wine on the label.

LIBRARY DUE-DATE CARDS

you will need

Mocha Cut-Out Cookies (page 25), large rectangle

Royal icing (page 29), divided and tinted:
IVORY • MEDIUM BLUE • BLACK

Disposable icing bags (3)

Couplers

Icing tips: #2, #1

Squeeze bottle

Toothpicks

Black gel paste food coloring

Uninked stamp pad (or stack of paper towels)

Unused date stamp

1 Scoop some ivory icing into a bag fitted with a #2 tip, and outline the rectangle. Ⓐ

2 Thin the ivory icing for flooding (see page 16). Cover it with a damp dishtowel and let it sit for several minutes. Gently stir it with a silicone spatula and transfer it to a squeeze bottle.
→ Fill in the outlined areas with the thinned icing. Use a toothpick to guide the icing to the edges and pop air bubbles. Ⓑ
→ Let the cookies dry for at least one hour.

3 Use a #2 tip with medium blue icing to pipe lines across the cookies. Ⓒ

4 Use a #1 tip with black icing to pipe the lettering across the top. Ⓓ
→ Let the cookies dry uncovered for 6 to 8 hours or overnight.

5 When the cookies are completely dry, stamp dates onto them with the date stamp and the food coloring-inked stamp pad (or paper towels) (see page 19). Gently press the stamp up, down, and back, to make a good impression. Don't worry if the stamping isn't perfect and appears patchy in some areas—it looks more realistic that way. Ⓔ

Note: Make sure you use a date stamp that has never been used with actual ink!

BOOKMARKS

you will need

Mocha Cut-Out Cookies (page 25), thin rectangle

Royal icing (page 29), divided and tinted:
MEDIUM BLUE • IVORY • GREEN

Disposable icing bags (3)

Couplers

Icing tips: #2

Squeeze bottle

Toothpicks

Drinking straw

Small flat paintbrush

Embroidery floss or ribbon

Note: Before baking, press a straw through the top of the cookie dough for a hole for the tassel. When you remove the cookies from the oven, press the straw back into the holes again in case they closed while baking.

1 Scoop some of the medium blue icing into a bag fitted with a #2 tip and outline the bookmark including around the hole for the ribbon. Ⓐ

2 Thin the blue icing for flooding (see page 16). Cover it with a damp dishtowel and let it sit for several minutes. Gently stir the icing with a silicone spatula and transfer it to a squeeze bottle.
→ Fill in the outlined area with the thinned icing. Use a toothpick to guide the icing to the edges and pop air bubbles. Ⓑ
→ Let the cookies dry uncovered for 6 to 8 hours or overnight.

3 Scoop some ivory icing into a bag fitted with a #2 tip, and outline the outer layer of petals. Use a flat paintbrush to decorate the outer layer using brush embroidery (see page 20).
→ Repeat, adding inner layers.
→ Use the same method to make leaves with the green icing, pulling the paintbrush towards the center of the leaf.
→ Use a #2 tip to add dots in the center of each flower in ivory, and a #2 tip to add a line down the center of each leaf in green icing. Ⓒ

4 When the cookies are completely dry, string embroidery floss tassels or ribbons through the holes.

les cosmos

les myosotis

les soucis

GARDEN PARTY

I may have a black thumb when it comes to actual gardening, but I can fake a green one in the kitchen! Inspired by vintage seed packets, these cookies feature simple renditions of some of my favorite flowers. Because we're fancy, the names are stamped in French. Ooh la la!

COSMOS (LES COSMOS)

les cosmos

you will need

Vanilla-Almond Sugar Cookies
(page 24), cut into a large
rectangle

White fondant

Corn syrup

Royal icing (page 29),
divided and tinted:
DEEP PINK • LIGHT PINK •
YELLOW • GREEN

Disposable icing bags (4)

Couplers

Icing tips: small star tips, #2, #1

Toothpicks

Uninked stamp pad (or stack of
paper towels)

Black gel paste food coloring

Alphabet stamps

1 Scoop each of the pink icings into bags. Use two small star tips for both
shades of pink to pipe the petals onto the fondant-covered cookie. Ⓐ

2 Use a #2 tip with yellow icing to pipe centers on the flowers.
→ Use a #2 tip with green icing to add the stems. Switch
to a #1 tip and add a few leaves. Ⓑ

3 Stamp the flower name onto the cookie using the black food coloring,
the uninked stamp pad (or paper towels), and the alphabet stamps (see
page 19). Ⓒ

Note: The base for all of these
cookie designs is fondant. Apply it as instructed on page 19.
If you prefer, the cookies can be
outlined and filled in with white
royal icing, which can serve as
the base instead of fondant.
Just make sure the royal icing is
completely dry before you add
the flower details.

STOCK (LES GIROFLÉES DES JARDINS)

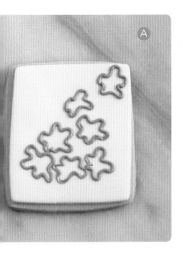

you will need

Vanilla-Almond Sugar Cookies
(page 24), cut into a large
rectangle

White fondant*

Corn syrup

Royal icing (page 29),
divided and tinted:
PURPLE • GREEN

Disposable icing bags (2)

Couplers

Icing tips: #2, #1, #3, leaf tip

Squeeze bottles (2)

Toothpicks

Uninked stamp pad (or stack of
paper towels)

Black gel paste food coloring

Alphabet stamps

*See page 59 for note on the
fondant base.

1 Scoop some purple icing into a bag fitted with a #2 tip, and pipe
small, squiggly-edged flowers across the fondant-covered cookie,
leaving some space between a few of the flowers. Ⓐ Reserve some of
the purple icing in the bag for piping details later.

2 Thin the purple icing for flooding (see page 16). Cover it with a
damp dishtowel and let it sit for several minutes. Gently stir it with a
silicone spatula and transfer it to a squeeze bottle.

→ Fill in the outlined areas with the thinned icing. Use a toothpick to
guide the icing to the edges and pop air bubbles. Ⓑ
→ Let the cookies dry for at least one hour.

3 Use a #1 tip with the purple icing to add detail piping to the flowers.
→ Use a #1 tip with green icing to add centers to the flowers. Switch to
a #2 tip and pipe a stem through the flowers. Switch to a #3 tip and
pipe the bottom part of the stem.
→ Use a leaf tip with green icing to pipe a long leaf on the side of the
bottom stem. Ⓒ

4 Stamp the flower name onto the cookie using the black food coloring, the uninked stamp pad (or paper towels), and the alphabet stamp
(see page 19). Ⓓ

POPPIES
(LES COQUELICOTS)

you will need

Vanilla-Almond Sugar Cookies (page 24), cut into a large rectangle

White fondant*

Corn syrup

Royal icing (page 29), divided and tinted:
RED • ELECTRIC GREEN • LEAF GREEN

Disposable icing bags (3)

Couplers

Icing tips: #2, #3

Paintbrushes, one flat and one small

Meringue powder

Black nonpareils

Uninked stamp pad (or stack of paper towels)

Black gel paste food coloring

Alphabet stamps

*See page 59 for note on the fondant base.

1 Scoop some red icing into a bag fitted with a #2 tip, and outline the outer layer of petals. Use a flat paintbrush to decorate the outer layer using brush embroidery (see page 20). Ⓐ

2 Repeat with the two inner layers. Ⓑ

3 Pipe on the following details:
→ Use a #3 tip with leaf green icing to add a stem.
→ Use a #3 tip with electric green icing to pipe a center on the poppy. Ⓒ
→ Let the icing dry for at least one hour.

4 Mix ¼ tablespoon meringue powder with ¼ teaspoon water. Use a small paintbrush to apply the mixture, dabbing it around the center of the flower. Sprinkle on the black nonpareils and shake off the excess. Ⓓ

5 Stamp the flower name onto the cookie using the black food coloring, the uninked stamp pad (or paper towels), and the alphabet stamp (see page 19).

MARIGOLDS
(LES SOUCIS)

you will need

Vanilla-Almond Sugar Cookies
(page 24), cut into a large
rectangle

White fondant*

Corn syrup

Royal icing (page 29),
divided and tinted:
ORANGE • YELLOW • GREEN

Disposable icing bags (3)

Couplers

Icing tips: #2, leaf

Squeeze bottles (2)

Toothpicks

Uninked stamp pad (or stack
of paper towels)

Black gel paste food coloring

Alphabet stamps

*See page 59 for note on the
fondant base.

1 Scoop some orange icing into a bag fitted with a #2 tip, and pipe a squiggly-edged circle onto the fondant-covered cookie. Do the same with the yellow icing and a #2 tip. Reserve both icings in their bags for piping details later. **Ⓐ**

2 Thin the orange and yellow icings for flooding (see page 16). Cover them with a damp dishtowel and let them sit for several minutes. Gently stir them with a silicone spatula and transfer them to squeeze bottles as needed.
→ Fill in the outlined areas with the thinned icing. Use a toothpick to guide the icing to the edges and pop air bubbles. **Ⓑ**
→ Let the cookies dry for at least one hour.

3 Pipe on the following details:
→ Use a #2 tip with the orange and yellow icings to pipe details onto the flowers. **Ⓒ**

4 Use a #2 tip with green icing to pipe stems and a leaf tip to add leaves. **Ⓓ**

5 Stamp the flower name onto the cookie using the black food coloring, the uninked stamp pad (or paper towels), and the alphabet stamp (see page 19). **Ⓔ**

FORGET-ME-NOTS
(LES MYOSOTIS)

you will need

Vanilla-Almond Sugar Cookies
(page 24) cut into a large rectangle

White fondant

Corn syrup

Royal icing (page 29), divided and
tinted:
BLUE • YELLOW • BLACK • GREEN

Disposable icing bags (4)

Couplers

Icing tips: Small and medium
petals, #2, #1

Waxed paper

Toothpicks

Uninked stamp pad (or stack of
paper towels)

Black gel paste food coloring

Alphabet stamps

*See page 59 for note on the
fondant base.

Note: Up to several weeks before you bake the cookies, pipe flowers in two sizes. On a sheet of waxed paper, pipe the petals of the flowers using small and medium petal tips with blue icing. To make each petal, hold the piping bag so that the wide end of the tip is closest to you and the small end is pointing up and to the left. The tip shouldn't touch the paper. Squeeze the bag while moving the tip slightly up and to the right. Touch the tip lightly at the end as you release the pressure. Rotate the wax paper and repeat the process to make five petals per flower. Ⓐ

→ Use a #2 tip with yellow icing to add a dot to the center of each flower.

→ Use a #1 tip with black icing to add a small center dot to each yellow dot. Ⓑ

→ Let the flowers dry for several hours or overnight. Then carefully peel away the waxed paper and transfer the piped flowers to an airtight container.

1 Use a bit of piping-consistency royal icing to adhere the pre-made flowers to the fondant-covered cookies when you're ready to decorate them.

2 Scoop some green icing into a bag fitted with a #2 tip, and add stems to each flower. Ⓒ

3 Stamp the flower name onto the cookie using the black food coloring, the uninked stamp pad (or paper towels), and the alphabet stamp (see page 19). Ⓓ

MONSTER MASH-UP

If you want to let the kids play with cookies but don't want a mess, let me introduce you to the Monster Mash-Up. Sure to elicit lots of giggles, the three members of this ghoulish trio are divided into thirds for lots of fun mixing and matching.

PURPLE MONSTERS

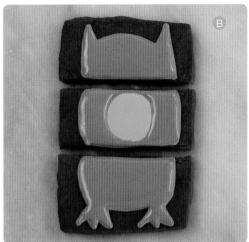

you will need

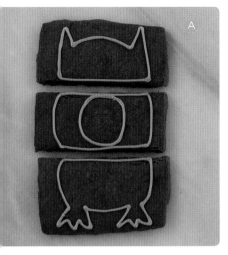

Gluten-Free Chocolate (or regular chocolate option) Cut-Out Cookies (page 28), rectangles

Bench scraper

Royal icing (page 29), divided and tinted:
ELECTRIC PURPLE •
ELECTRIC GREEN •
ORANGE • WHITE • BLACK

Disposable icing bags (5)

Couplers

Icing tips: #2, #1

Squeeze bottles (3)

Toothpicks

Note: Immediately after you remove the cookies from the oven, use a bench scraper to cut each cookie into even thirds.

1 Scoop some of the electric purple icing into a bag fitted with a #2 tip, and outline the head, torso, and bottom of the monster. Section off a circle in the middle of the torso. Ⓐ Reserve some of the icing in the bag for piping details later.

2 Thin the purple, green, and orange icings for flooding (see page 16). Cover them with a damp dishtowel and let them sit for several minutes. Gently stir them with a silicone spatula and transfer them to squeeze bottles as needed.
→ Fill in the outlined areas with the thinned purple icing. Use a toothpick to guide the icing to the edges and pop air bubbles. Working 6 to 8 cookies at a time, fill in the center circle section of each monster with the thinned green icing. Ⓑ
→ Beginning with the cookies you filled first, add dots of orange on top of the wet green icing (see page 18, Flood-on-Flood).
→ Let the cookies dry for at least one hour.

3 Thin the white icing using the 12- to 15-second method described in step 3 on page 16. Cover it with a damp dishtowel and let it sit for several minutes. Gently stir it with a silicone spatula and transfer it to a bag fitted with a #2 tip. Pipe eyes onto the face.

4 Thin the black icing with several drops of water, stirring it well so that it doesn't come to a stiff point. Transfer the icing to a bag fitted with a #1 tip, and pipe pupils onto the eyes.

5 Use a #1 tip with purple icing to add arms. Use #1 tips to add a tail, mouth and teeth with orange and green icing. Ⓒ
→ Let the cookies dry uncovered for 6 to 8 hours or overnight.

GREEN MONSTERS

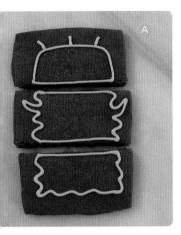

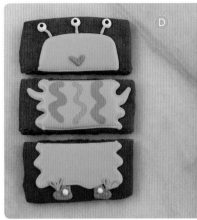

you will need

Gluten-Free Chocolate (or regular chocolate option) Cut-Out Cookies (page 28), rectangles

Bench scraper

Royal icing (page 29), divided and tinted:
ORANGE • ELECTRIC PURPLE • ELECTRIC GREEN • WHITE • BLACK

Disposable icing bags (5)

Couplers

Icing tips: #2, #3, #1

Squeeze bottles (3)

Toothpicks

Note: Immediately after you remove the cookies from the oven, use a bench scraper to cut each cookie into even thirds.

1 Scoop some of the electric green icing into a bag fitted with a #2 tip, and outline the head, torso, and bottom of the monsters. Ⓐ

2 Thin the green, purple, and orange icings for flooding (see page 16). Cover them with a damp dishtowel and let them sit for several minutes. Gently stir them with a silicone spatula and transfer them to squeeze bottles as needed.
→ Fill in the outlines on the head and bottom only with the thinned green icing. Use a toothpick to guide the icing to the edges and pop air bubbles.

3 Working 6 to 8 cookies at a time, fill in the torso with the thinned green icing. Ⓑ
→ Beginning with the cookies you filled first, add squiggly lines of purple and orange on top of the wet green icing. Ⓒ
→ Let the cookies dry for at least one hour.

4 Use a #2 tip to pipe high-top shoes with purple icing. Add a heart-shaped mouth.

5 Use a # 1 tip with orange icing to add laces to the shoes.

6 Thin the white icing using the 12- to 15-second method described on page 16. Cover it with a damp dishtowel and let it sit for several minutes. Gently stir it with a silicone spatula and transfer it to a bag fitted with a #2 tip. Pipe eyes onto the face.

7 Switch to a #1 tip and add dots to the shoes.
→ Use a #1 tip with black icing to add pupils to the eyes. Ⓓ
→ Let the cookies dry uncovered for 6 to 8 hours or overnight.

ORANGE MONSTERS

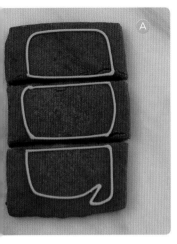
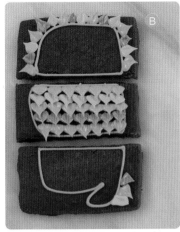
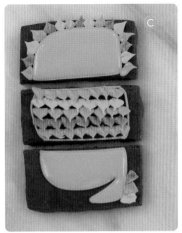
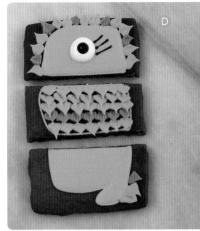

you will need

Gluten-Free Chocolate (or regular chocolate option) Cut-Out Cookies (page 28), rectangles

Bench scraper

Royal icing (page 29), divided and tinted:
ORANGE • ELECTRIC PURPLE • ELECTRIC GREEN • WHITE • BLACK

Disposable icing bags (5)

Couplers

Icing tips: #2, leaf, 1, 3, 7

Squeeze bottle

Toothpicks

Note: Immediately after you remove the cookies from the oven, use the bench scraper to cut each cookie into even thirds.

1 Scoop some of the orange icing into a bag fitted with a # 2 tip, and outline the head, torso, and bottom of the monster. (A)

2 Use the leaf tip and with the orange, purple, and green icings to pipe spikes on the top of the head, the tail, and across the monster's torso. (B)

3 Thin the orange icing for flooding (see page 16). Cover it with a damp dishtowel and let it sit for several minutes. Gently stir it with a silicone spatula and transfer it to a squeeze bottle.
→ Fill in the outlined areas with the thinned icing. Use a toothpick to guide the icing to the edges and pop air bubbles. (C)
→ Let the cookies dry for at least one hour.

4 Thin the white icing using the 12- to 15-second method described on page 16. Cover it with a damp dishtowel and let it sit for several minutes. Gently stir it with a silicone spatula and transfer it to a piping bag fitted with a #7 tip. Pipe an eye in the center of the face.

5 Use a #1 tip with black icing to add eyelashes. Squeeze the icing back into a bowl. Thin the black icing with several drops of water, stirring it well so that it doesn't come to a stiff point. Transfer it back to a bag, attach a #3 tip, and pipe a pupil on the eye. (D)
→ Let the cookies dry uncovered for 6 to 8 hours or overnight.

OUTER SPACE

For an otherworldly cookie experience, break out the sparkle, the shimmer...and the aliens.

MOONS

you will need

Gluten-Free Chocolate (or regular chocolate option) Cut-Out Cookies (page 28), circles

Cornstarch

White fondant

Corn syrup

Chopstick

Paintbrush

Silver luster dust

1 On a work surface dusted with cornstarch, roll out the white fondant to a thickness of ⅛ inch. Cut it with the same cookie cutter you used for the cookies.

2 Brush the tops of the cookies with corn syrup and place the cut fondant pieces on top. Ⓐ

3 Use the ends of a chopstick to press "craters" into the fondant. If your chopstick isn't rounded on the end, don't worry. Simply twirl the chopstick to make round indentions. Ⓑ

4 Use a dry paintbrush to apply silver luster dust directly onto the fondant.

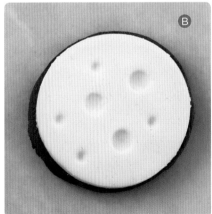

ROCKETS

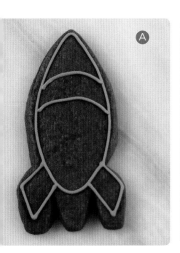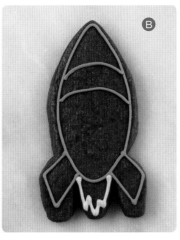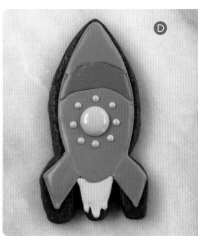

you will need

Gluten-Free Chocolate
(or regular chocolate option)
Cut-Out Cookies (page 28),
rocket shape

Royal icing (page 29),
divided and tinted:
ROYAL BLUE • YELLOW •
RED • GRAY

Disposable icing bags (4)

Couplers

Icing tips: #2, #4, #1

Squeeze bottles (3)

Toothpicks

Silver luster dust

Vodka

Paintbrush

Food-coloring pens in red
and orange

1 Scoop some of the royal blue icing into a bag fitted with a #2 tip, and outline the rocket body and legs. Reserve some of this icing in the bag for piping details later. Ⓐ

2 Scoop some of the yellow icing into a bag, attach a #2 tip, and outline the flames of the rocket. Ⓑ

3 Set aside some red piping-consistency icing before you thin it. Thin the blue, yellow, and red icings for flooding (see page 16). Cover them with a damp dishtowel and let them sit for several minutes. Gently stir them with a silicone spatula and transfer them to squeeze bottles as needed.

→ Fill in the outlined areas with the thinned icing. Use a toothpick to guide the icing to the edges and pop air bubbles. Ⓒ

→ Let the cookies dry for at least one hour.

4 Thin most of the gray icing and the remaining red icing using the 12- to 15-second method described in step 3 on page 16. Cover them with a damp dishtowel and let them sit for several minutes. Gently stir them with a silicone spatula and transfer them to bags.

→ Use a #4 tip with gray icing to pipe a window in the center of the rocket. Swirl the icing lightly with a toothpick to loosen any air bubbles.

→ Switch to a #1 tip and pipe dots around the window. Ⓓ

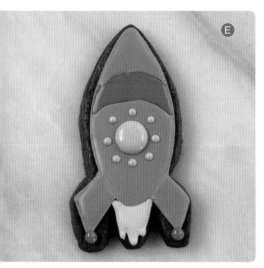

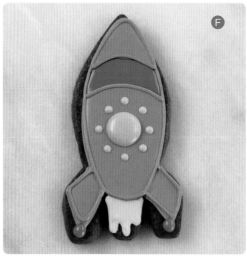

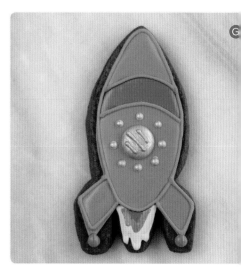

→ Use a #2 tip with red icing to pipe dots to accent the rocket legs. Ⓔ

→ Use a #2 tip with royal blue icing to outline the entire rocket. Ⓕ

→ Use a #1 tip with the gray icing to add detail lines across the window.

→ Let the cookies dry uncovered for 6 to 8 hours or overnight.

5 When the cookies are dry, mix ¼ teaspoon of the silver luster dust with the vodka until smooth. Use a paintbrush to apply this mixture to the rocket window and gray dots.

6 Use the red and orange food-coloring pens to add details on top of the yellow flames. Ⓖ

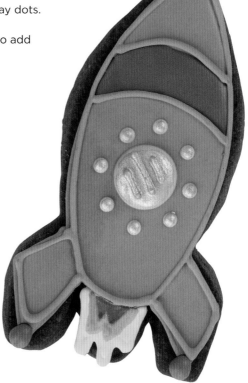

SWIRLY PLANETS

you will need

Gluten-Free Chocolate (or regular chocolate option) Cut-Out Cookies (page 28), circles

Royal icing (page 29), divided and tinted:
ELECTRIC GREEN • RED • BLUE • ORANGE • YELLOW

Disposable icing bag

Couplers

Icing tips: #2

Toothpicks

Squeeze bottles (5)

1 Scoop some of the green icing into a bag fitted with a #2 tip, and outline the circle. Ⓐ

2 Thin the green, red, blue, orange, and yellow icings for flooding (see page 16). Cover them with a damp dishtowel and let them sit for several minutes. Gently stir them with a silicone spatula and transfer them to squeeze bottles.

→ Working 6 to 8 cookies at a time, fill in the outlined areas with the thinned green icing. Use a toothpick to guide the icing to the edges and pop air bubbles. Beginning with the first cookie you flooded, add swirls and lines using the thinned red, blue, orange, and yellow icings across the wet green icing. Ⓑ

→ Let the cookies dry uncovered for 6 to 8 hours or overnight.

SPACESHIPS

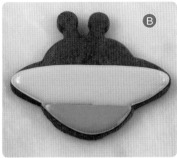
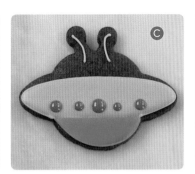
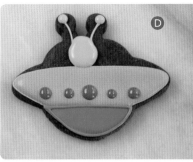

you will need

> Gluten-Free Chocolate (or regular chocolate option) Cut-Out Cookies (page 28), spaceship shape
>
> Royal icing (page 29), divided and tinted:
> ROYAL BLUE • GRAY • ELECTRIC GREEN • RED
>
> Disposable icing bags (5)
>
> Couplers
>
> Icing tips: #2, #1, #3
>
> Squeeze bottles (2)
>
> Toothpicks
>
> Silver luster dust
>
> Vodka
>
> Paintbrush
>
> Black food-coloring pen

1 Scoop some of the royal blue icing into a bag fitted with a #2 tip, and outline the base of the spaceship. Reserve some of this icing in the bag for piping details later. Scoop some of the gray icing into a bag, attach a #2 tip, and outline the middle of the spaceship. Ⓐ

2 Thin the blue and gray icings for flooding (see page 16). Cover them with a damp dishtowel and let them sit for several minutes. Gently stir them with a silicone spatula and transfer them to squeeze bottles as needed.
→ Fill in the outlined areas with the thinned icing. Use a toothpick to guide the icing to the edges and pop air bubbles. Ⓑ

3 Thin the red icing using the 12- to 15-second method described in step 3 on page 16. Cover it with a damp dishtowel and let it sit for several minutes. Gently stir it with a silicone spatula and transfer it to a bag fitted with a #3 tip. Add red dots along the bottom of the silver section of the spaceship. Swirl the icing lightly with a toothpick to loosen any air bubbles.

4 Scoop some electric green icing into a bag, attach a #1 tip, and pipe antennae stems for the aliens. Ⓒ

5 Repeat step 3 using the electric green icing to pipe a head for the alien and circles for the antennae. Swirl the icing lightly with a toothpick to loosen any air bubbles. Ⓓ
→ Let the cookies dry for at least one hour.

6 Use a #2 tip with blue icing to outline the bottom of the spaceship.
→ Let the cookies dry uncovered for 6 to 8 hours or overnight.

7 When the cookies are dry, mix ¼ teaspoon of the silver luster dust with the vodka until smooth. Use a paintbrush to apply the mixture to the gray section of the spaceship. Use the black food-coloring pen to give the alien eyes and a smile.

RINGED PLANETS

you will need

Gluten-Free Chocolate (or regular chocolate option) Cut-Out Cookies (page 28), circles

Royal icing (page 29), divided and tinted:
ROYAL BLUE • YELLOW • RED

Disposable icing bags (2)

Couplers

Icing tips: #2, #1, #7

Squeeze bottles (2)

Toothpicks

Note: Before you bake the cookies, or as soon as they come out of the oven, press a smaller circle cookie cutter into the dough to create a template for piping circles. Ⓐ

Tip: Circles are notoriously difficult to pipe perfectly. Use a guide when you can and be sure to let the icing drop onto the cookie outline—don't drag it across. My own circles are rarely, if ever, perfect. Repeat after me: "It's only a cookie."

1 Scoop some of the royal blue icing into a bag fitted with a #2 tip, and outline the planet following the imprint on the cookie. Ⓑ

2 Thin the blue and yellow icings for flooding (see page 16). Cover them with a damp dishtowel and let them sit for several minutes. Gently stir them with a silicone spatula and transfer them to squeeze bottles as needed.
→ Working 6 to 8 cookies at a time, fill in the outlined areas with the thinned blue icing. Use a toothpick to guide the icing to the edges and pop air bubbles. Ⓒ

3 Beginning with the first cookie you flooded, add yellow dots on top of the wet blue icing (see page 18, Flood-on-Flood). Ⓓ
→ Let the cookies dry for at least one hour.

4 Thin the red icing using the 12- to 15-second method described in step 3 on page 16. Cover it with a damp dishtowel and let it sit for several minutes. Gently stir it with a silicone spatula and transfer it to a piping bag fitted with a #7 tip.
→ Pipe a ring around the planet. Ⓔ
→ Let the cookies dry uncovered for 6 to 8 hours or overnight.

METEORS

PAGE
86

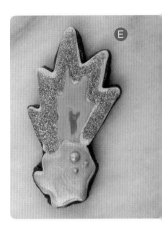

you will need

Gluten-Free Chocolate (or regular chocolate option) Cut-Out Cookies (page 28), meteor shape (template, page 143)

Royal icing (page 29), divided and tinted:
GRAY • RED • ORANGE • YELLOW

Disposable icing bags (3)

Couplers

Icing tips: #2, #1

Squeeze bottles (4)

Toothpicks

Paintbrushes

Silver luster dust

Meringue powder

Gold disco dust

1 Scoop some of the gray icing into a bag fitted with a #2 tip, and outline the meteor. Reserve some of this icing in the bag for piping details later. Ⓐ

2 Scoop some of the yellow and orange icings into bags. Use #2 tips with each to outline and section off the flame. Ⓑ

3 Thin the gray, red, orange, and yellow icings for flooding (see page 16). Cover them with a damp dishtowel and let them sit for several minutes. Gently stir them with a silicone spatula and transfer them to squeeze bottles as needed.
→ Fill in the outlined areas with the thinned icing. Use a toothpick to guide icing to the edges and pop air bubbles. Ⓒ

4 Use a #1 tip with gray icing to pipe details onto the meteor. Ⓓ
→ Let the cookies dry uncovered for 6 to 8 hours or overnight.

5 When the cookies are dry, brush silver luster dust onto the gray section of the meteor using the dry application method described on page 21.

6 Mix ¼ teaspoon meringue powder with ¼ teaspoon water. With a small paintbrush, apply the mixture to the yellow portion of the flame. Sprinkle on the gold disco dust and shake off the excess (see page 21 for details on applying disco dust). Ⓔ

PRINCESS

Fancy dress? Check. Princess hat? Check. Frog prince, carriage, and white horse? Check, check, and check! These princess cookies go from simply pretty to utterly magical in an instant thanks to a smattering of disco dust.

PRINCESS HATS

you will need

Vanilla-Almond Sugar Cookies
(page 24), princess hat shape

Royal icing (page 29),
divided and tinted:
PURPLE (LIGHT AND DARK
SHADES) • YELLOW

Disposable icing bag

Couplers

Icing tip: #3

Squeeze bottles (3)

Toothpicks

Meringue powder

Paintbrushes

Rainbow disco dust

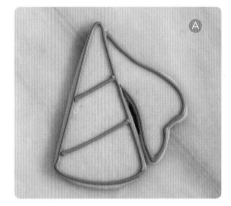

1 Scoop some dark purple icing into a bag fitted with a #3 tip, and outline the cookies. Section off the areas that will be filled in with different colors, including the veil. Ⓐ

2 Thin the dark purple, light purple, and yellow icings for flooding (see page 16). Cover them with a damp dishtowel and let them sit for several minutes. Gently stir them with a silicone spatula and transfer them to squeeze bottles as needed.
→ Fill in the outlined areas with the thinned icing. Use a toothpick to guide the icing to the edges and pop air bubbles. Ⓑ
→ Let the cookies dry uncovered for 6 to 8 hours or overnight.

3 When the cookies are dry, mix ½ teaspoon of meringue powder with ½ teaspoon of water. Use the paintbrush to apply this mixture to the veil. Sprinkle on the disco dust and shake off the excess (see page 21 for details on applying disco dust). Use a dry paintbrush to brush stray sparkles off the cookies.

PRINCESS DRESSES

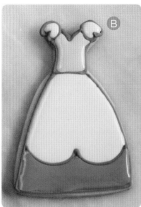
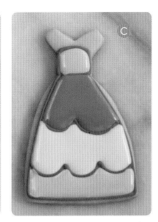

you will need

Vanilla-Almond Sugar Cookies
(page 24), princess dress shape

Royal icing (page 29),
divided and tinted:
PURPLE (LIGHT AND DARK SHADES) •
YELLOW

Disposable icing bag

Couplers

Icing tips: #3, #2

Squeeze bottles (3)

Toothpicks

Meringue powder

Paintbrushes

Rainbow disco dust

1 Scoop some dark purple icing into a bag fitted with a #3 tip, and outline the cookies. Section off the areas that will be filled in with different colors. Reserve some of the dark purple icing in the bag for piping details later. Ⓐ

2 Thin the dark purple, light purple, and yellow icings for flooding (see page 16).
Cover them with a damp dishtowel and let them sit for several minutes. Gently stir them with a silicone spatula and transfer them to squeeze bottles as needed.
→ Fill in the outlined areas with the thinned icing. Use a toothpick to guide the icing to the edges and pop air bubbles. Ⓑ and Ⓒ
→ Let the cookies dry for at least one hour.

3 Use a #2 tip with dark purple icing to add detailing to the dresses. Ⓓ and Ⓔ
→ Let the cookies dry uncovered for 6 to 8 hours or overnight.

4 When the cookies are dry, mix ½ teaspoon of meringue powder with ½ teaspoon of water. Use the paintbrush to apply this mixture to the cookies in the areas where you want the disco dust to stick. Sprinkle on the disco dust and shake off the excess (see page 21 for details on applying disco dust). Use a dry paintbrush to brush stray sparkles off the cookies.

CASTLES

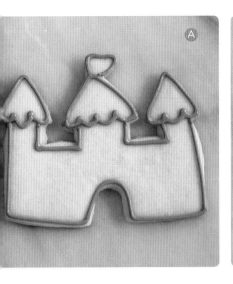

you will need

Vanilla-Almond Sugar Cookies (page 24), castle shape

Royal icing (page 29), divided and tinted: PURPLE (LIGHT AND DARK SHADES) • YELLOW

Disposable icing bag

Couplers

Icing tips: #3, #2

Squeeze bottles (3)

Toothpicks

Meringue powder

Paintbrushes

Rainbow disco dust

1 Scoop some dark purple icing into a bag fitted with a #3 tip, and outline the cookies. Reserve some of the icing in the bag for piping details later. A

2 Thin the yellow, dark purple, and light purple icings for flooding (see page 16). Cover them with a damp dishtowel and let them sit for several minutes. Gently stir them with a silicone spatula and transfer them to squeeze bottles as needed.
→ Fill in the outlined areas with thinned icing as follows, using a toothpick to guide the icing to the edges and pop air bubbles:
→ Use yellow icing to fill in the base of the castle.
→ Use dark purple icing to fill in the flag.
→ Use light purple icing to fill in the turrets. B

3 Use a #2 tip with dark purple icing to pipe over the outlines of the turrets and add lines to the middle one. Pipe a scalloped line across the middle of the castle. C
→ Let the cookies dry uncovered for 6 to 8 hours or overnight.

4 When the cookies are dry, mix ½ teaspoon meringue powder with ½ teaspoon water. Use the paintbrush to apply this mixture to the turrets. Sprinkle on the disco dust and shake off the excess (see page 21 for details on applying disco dust). Use a dry paintbrush to brush stray sparkles off the cookies.

CARRIAGES

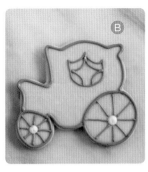

you will need

Vanilla-Almond Sugar Cookies (page 24), carriage shape

Royal icing (page 29), divided and tinted:
YELLOW • DARK PURPLE • WHITE • GREEN

Disposable icing bags (3)

Couplers

Icing tips: #4, #3, #2, #1

Squeeze bottles (3)

Toothpicks

Meringue powder

Paintbrushes

Rainbow disco dust

1 Scoop some yellow icing into a bag fitted with a #4 tip, and pipe a circle for a rose in the center of each wheel. Reserve some of the icing in the bag for piping details later. Ⓐ

2 Scoop some dark purple icing into a bag, attach a #4 tip, and pipe circles for the wheels.
→ Switch to a #3 tip and outline the main section of the carriage.
→ Switch to a #2 tip and outline the window and curtains, and add spokes to the wheels. Reserve some of the icing in the bag for piping details later. Ⓑ

3 Thin the dark purple, white, and yellow icings for flooding (see page 16). Cover them with a damp dishtowel and let them sit for several minutes. Gently stir them with a silicone spatula and transfer them to squeeze bottles as needed.
→ Fill in the outlined areas with thinned icing as follows, using a toothpick to guide the icing to the edges and pop air bubbles:
→ Use white icing to fill in the main section of the carriage.
→ Use yellow icing to fill in the window.
→ Use purple icing to fill in the curtains. Ⓒ
→ Let the cookies dry for at least one hour.

4 Use a #4 tip with the yellow icing to pipe a rose over the top of the window. Ⓓ
→ Use a #2 tip with dark purple icing to go over the outline of the main part of the carriage. Switch to a #1 tip and add details to the center of the roses, the curtains, and add two dots on each side of the rose above the window.
→ Use a #1 tip with the green icing to add leaves to the flowers. Ⓔ
→ Let the cookies dry uncovered for 6 to 8 hours or overnight.

5 When the cookies are dry, mix ½ teaspoon of meringue powder with ½ teaspoon of water. Use the paintbrush to apply this mixture to the window. Sprinkle on the disco dust and shake off the excess (see page 21 for details on applying disco dust). Use a dry paintbrush to brush stray sparkles off the cookies.

HORSES

you will need

Vanilla-Almond
Sugar Cookies (page
24), horse shape

Royal icing (page 29),
divided and tinted:
PURPLE (LIGHT AND
DARK SHADES) • WHITE •
YELLOW • GREEN

Disposable icing bags (3)

Couplers

Icing tips: #2, #3, #1

Squeeze bottles (3)

Toothpicks

Meringue powder

Paintbrushes

Rainbow disco dust

Black food-coloring pen

1 Scoop some of the dark purple icing into a bag fitted with a #2 tip, and outline the horse. Section off areas for the tail, mane, saddle, and hooves. Fill in the hooves using a back and forth motion with the icing. Reserve some of the icing in the bag for piping details later. Ⓐ

2 Thin the dark purple, white, and light purple icings for flooding (see page 16). Cover them with a damp dishtowel and let them sit for several minutes. Gently stir them with a silicone spatula and transfer them to squeeze bottles as needed.
→ Fill in the outlined areas with thinned icing as follows, using a toothpick to guide the icing to the edges and pop air bubbles:
→ Use white icing to fill in the body of the horse.
→ Use dark purple icing to fill in the tail and mane.
→ Use light purple icing to fill in the saddle. Ⓑ
→ Let the cookies dry for at least one hour.

3 Use a #2 tip with dark purple icing to pipe a forelock across the top of the horse's head. Flood the forelock with the thinned dark purple icing. Use a toothpick to guide the icing to the edges and pop air bubbles.
→ Use a #3 tip with yellow icing to pipe roses on the saddle and mane of the horse.
→ Use a #1 tip with dark purple icing to add details to the roses, tail, and mane. Add a bridle to the horse.
→ Use a #1 tip with green icing to add leaves to the flowers. Ⓒ
→ Let the cookies dry uncovered for 6 to 8 hours or overnight.

4 When the cookies are dry, mix ½ teaspoon of meringue powder with ½ teaspoon of water. Use the paintbrush to apply this mixture to the saddle, going around the roses. Sprinkle on the disco dust and shake off the excess (see page 21 for details on applying disco dust). Use a dry paintbrush to brush stray sparkles off the cookies.

5 Use the black food-coloring pen to give the horse an eye and eyelashes.

PRINCESS FACE COOKIES

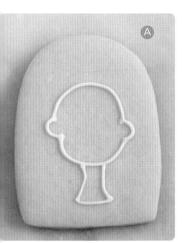   

you will need

Vanilla-Almond Sugar Cookies
(page 24), princess face shape

Royal icing (page 29),
divided and tinted:
COPPER • BROWN • GOLD •
PURPLE • PINK • GREEN

Disposable icing bags (6)

Couplers

Icing tips: #2, #1

Squeeze bottles (2)

Toothpicks

Tweezers

Sugar pearls

Food-coloring pens in pink,
brown, and black

Meringue powder

Small paintbrush

Rainbow disco dust

Note: Feel free to change the hair and eye colors for your princess cookies. For darker skin tones, swap the copper food coloring for warm brown.

1 Scoop some of the copper icing into a bag fitted with a #2 tip, and outline the face and neck. Ⓐ

2 Thin the copper icing for flooding (see page 16). Cover it with a damp dishtowel and let it sit for several minutes. Gently stir it with a silicone spatula and transfer it to a squeeze bottle.
→ Fill in the outlined areas with the thinned icing. Use a toothpick to guide the icing to the edges and pop air bubbles.
→ Use tweezers to place sugar pearls across the neck. Ⓑ
→ Let the cookies dry for at least one hour.

3 Use a #2 tip to outline the hair in brown icing. Ⓒ

4 Reserve some of the piping consistency icing for piping details later. Thin the brown icing for flooding (see page 16). Cover it with a damp dishtowel and let it sit for several minutes. Gently stir it with a silicone spatula and transfer it to a squeeze bottle.
→ Fill in the outlined areas with the thinned icing. Use a toothpick to guide the icing to the edges and pop air bubbles.
→ Use tweezers to place sugar pearls below each ear. Ⓓ
→ Let the cookies dry for at least one hour.

5 Pipe on the following details:

→ Use a #2 tip with gold icing to add a crown.

→ Use a #1 tip with purple icing to add details to the crown. Ⓔ

6 Use a #2 tip with pink icing to add a heart-shaped mouth.

→ Use a #1 tip with green icing to add eyes.

→ Use a #1 tip with brown icing to add hair details. Ⓕ

→ Let the cookies dry uncovered for 6 to 8 hours or overnight.

7 When the cookies are dry, add the rest of the facial details:

→ Use a pink food-coloring pen to add pink cheeks, a brown pen to add freckles, and a black pen to add eyelashes.

8 Mix ¼ teaspoon meringue powder with ¼ teaspoon water. Use a small paintbrush to apply the mixture to the purple portion of the crown. Sprinkle on the rainbow disco dust and shake off the excess (see page 21 for details on applying disco dust).

FROG PRINCES

you will need

Vanilla-Almond Sugar Cookies (page 24), frog prince shape

Royal icing (page 29), divided and tinted:

DARK PURPLE • YELLOW • GREEN (LIGHT AND DARK SHADES)

Disposable icing bags (2)

Couplers

Icing tips: #3

Squeeze bottles (4)

Toothpicks

Large heart-shaped sprinkles

Meringue powder

Paintbrushes

Rainbow disco dust

Black food-coloring pen

1 Scoop some of the dark purple icing into a bag fitted with a #3 tip, and outline all sections of the frog.

2 Thin the dark purple, yellow, dark and light green icings for flooding (see page 16). Cover them with a damp dishtowel and let them sit for several minutes. Gently stir them with a silicone spatula and transfer them to squeeze bottles as needed.
→ Fill in the outlined areas with the thinned icing. Use a toothpick to guide the icing to the edges and pop air bubbles.
→ Let the cookies dry for at least one hour.

3 Use a #1 tip to pipe a bit of icing onto one side of a heart-shaped sprinkle and gently press the sprinkle onto the tummy of the frog.
→ Use a #1 tip with dark green icing to add arms and fingers to the frog.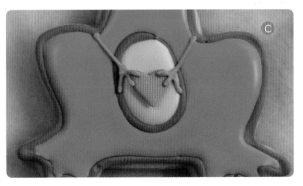

4 When the cookies are dry, mix ½ teaspoon of meringue powder with ½ teaspoon of water. Use a paintbrush to apply this mixture to the crown. Sprinkle on the disco dust and shake off the excess (see page 21 for details on applying disco dust). Use a dry paintbrush to brush stray sparkles off the cookies.

5 Use the black food-coloring pen to give the frog prince eyes and a smile.

TAILGATE

Customizable for any football team, these cookies are sure to score points at a tailgate party, Super Bowl celebration, or end-of-season bash. We all know that football and food go hand in hand. Rah, rah, sis-boom… COOKIE!

FOOTBALLS

you will need

Brown Sugar and Spice Cookies (page 26), football shape

Royal icing (page 29), divided and tinted:
BROWN • WHITE

Disposable icing bags (2)

Couplers

Icing tips: #2, #1

Squeeze bottles (2)

Toothpicks

1 Scoop some brown icing into a bag fitted with a #2 tip, and outline the football.

2 Scoop some white icing into a bag fitted with a #2 tip, and section off areas on each end of the ball for filling in with white icing.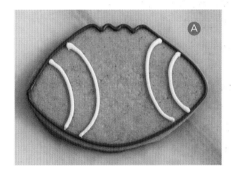

3 Before thinning, reserve some brown piping-consistency icing and some white piping-consistency icing in bags for piping details later. Thin the brown and white icings for flooding (see page 16). Cover them with a damp dishtowel and let them sit for several minutes. Gently stir them with a silicone spatula and transfer them to squeeze bottles.
→ Fill in the outlined areas with the thinned icing. Use a toothpick to guide the icing to the edges and pop air bubbles.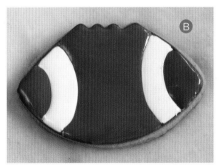
→ Let the cookies dry for at least one hour.

4 Use a #2 tip with white icing to add lacing details.
→ Use a #1 tip with brown icing to add details.
→ Let the cookies dry uncovered for 6 to 8 hours or overnight.

HELMETS

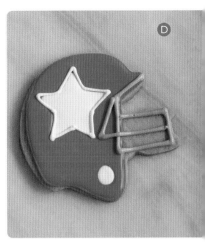

you will need

Brown Sugar and Spice Cookies (page 26), helmet shape, small star shape

Royal icing (page 29), divided and tinted:
RED • WHITE • GRAY

Disposable icing bags (3)

Couplers

Icing tips: #2, #1, #4

Squeeze bottles (2)

Toothpicks

Silver luster dust

Vodka

Small paintbrush

Note: Before baking, or immediately after removing from the oven, press a small star cookie cutter lightly into the cut dough to use as a guide for piping (see page 20).

1 Scoop some red icing into a bag fitted with a #2 tip, and outline the helmet, star, and small circle. Ⓐ

2 Reserve some white piping-consistency icing for piping details later. Thin the red and white icings for flooding (as described on page 16). Cover them with a damp dishtowel and let them sit for several minutes. Gently stir them with a silicone spatula and transfer them to squeeze bottles.
➜ Fill in the outlined areas with the thinned icing. Use a toothpick to guide the icing to the edges and pop air bubbles. Ⓑ
➜ Let the cookies dry for at least one hour.

3 Use a #1 or #2 tip with white icing to outline the star. Ⓒ

4 Use a #4 tip with gray icing to pipe the helmet facemask bars. Ⓓ
➜ Let the cookies dry uncovered for 6-8 hours or overnight.

5 When the cookies are dry, mix ¼ teaspoon silver luster dust with several drops of vodka until smooth. Use a small, clean paintbrush to apply the mixture to the gray piping.

REFEREE SHIRTS

you will need

Brown Sugar and Spice Cookies
(page 26), shirt shape

Royal icing (page 29),
divided and tinted:
WHITE • BLACK

Disposable icing bags (2)

Couplers

Icing tips: #2, #4, #1

Squeeze bottle

Toothpicks

1 Scoop some white icing into a bag fitted with a #2 tip, and outline the shirt. Ⓐ

2 Thin the white icing for flooding (see page 16). Cover it with a damp dishtowel and let it sit for several minutes. Gently stir it with a silicone spatula and transfer it to a squeeze bottle.
→ Fill in the outlined areas with the thinned icing. Use a toothpick to guide the icing to the edges and pop air bubbles. Ⓑ
→ Let the cookies dry for at least one hour.

3 Use a #1 tip with black icing to pipe the details onto the shirt. Pipe two lines next to each other on the edge of each sleeve. Pipe two tilted rectangles for the collar and fill them in with more piping. Ⓒ

4 Pipe lines down the shirt and across the sleeves. Add a pocket and fill it with piping-consistency icing. Ⓓ
→ Let the cookies dry uncovered for 6 to 8 hours or overnight.

MEGAPHONES

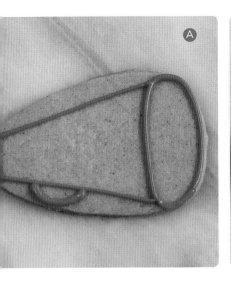

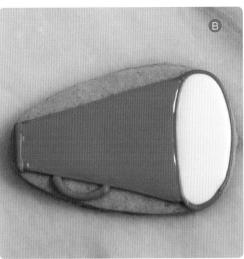

you will need

Brown Sugar and Spice Cookies (page 26), megaphone shape (made with a candy-corn cookie cutter)

Royal icing (page 29), divided and tinted:
RED • WHITE • BLACK

Disposable icing bags (3)

Couplers

Icing tips: #4, #2, #1

Squeeze bottles (2)

Toothpicks

1 Scoop some red icing into a bag fitted with a #4 tip, and pipe an oval at the large end of the megaphone and a line for the mouthpiece. Switch to a #2 tip and pipe the outline of the megaphone. Switch back to the #4 tip and add a handle. Ⓐ

2 Reserve some white piping-consistency icing before thinning for piping details later. Thin the red and white icings for flooding (see page 16). Cover them with a damp dishtowel and let them sit for several minutes. Gently stir them with a silicone spatula and transfer them to squeeze bottles as needed.
→ Fill in the outlined areas with the thinned icing. Use a toothpick to guide the icing to the edges and pop air bubbles. Ⓑ
→ Let the cookies dry for at least one hour.

3 Use a #2 tip with white icing to add details to the white oval.

4 Use a #1 tip with black icing to pipe the word "CHEER" across the body of the megaphone. Tip: If you're nervous about piping letters, practice on a plate or sheet of waxed paper before you decorate the cookies. Ⓒ
→ Let the cookies dry uncovered for 6 to 8 hours or overnight.

TAILGATE

FOAM FINGERS

you will need

Brown Sugar and Spice Cookies
(page 26), foam finger shape

Royal icing (page 29),
divided and tinted:
RED • WHITE • BLACK

Disposable icing bags (3)

Couplers

Icing tips: #2, #1

Squeeze bottles (2)

Toothpicks

1 Scoop some white icing into a bag fitted with a #2 tip, and outline the foam finger. Ⓐ

2 Before thinning, reserve some white piping-consistency icing in bags for piping details later. Thin the white icing for flooding (see page 16). Cover it with a damp dishtowel and let it sit for several minutes. Gently stir it with a silicone spatula and transfer it to a squeeze bottle.
→ Fill in the outlines with the thinned icing. Use a toothpick to guide the icing to the edges and pop air bubbles. Ⓑ
→ Let the cookies dry at least 1 hour.
→ Use a #1 tip to pipe a "#" onto the finger with black icing. Switch the tip to a #2, and outline the shape of a 1. Because we're filling in a black outline with another color, let the outline dry for at least one hour. Ⓒ

3 Thin the red icing for flooding (see page 16). Cover it with a damp dishtowel and let it sit for several minutes. Gently stir it with a silicone spatula and transfer it to a squeeze bottle.
→ Fill in the outline with the thinned icing. Use a toothpick to guide the icing to the edges and pop air bubbles. Ⓓ
Note: take care not to overfill the small area with thinned icing as this can lead to cratering.
→ Use a #2 tip to pipe a detail line on the finger with white icing.
→ Let the cookies dry uncovered for 6 to 8 hours or overnight.

UNDER THE SEA

A simple design is key to making sure kids (and adults) enjoy the process of cookie decorating. Let little ones come up with their own color combinations, add their own sprinkles, and, of course, do some taste testing along the way. Googly eyes guarantee cookies with personality. You can buy them pre-packaged at your local grocery or craft store or pipe them yourself. If you and the kiddos are making these cookies together, be sure to check out the helpful hints on page 32.

STARFISH

you will need

Pink Lemonade Cut-Out Cookies
(page 27), starfish shape

Royal icing (page 29),
divided and tinted:
ELECTRIC YELLOW (LIGHT AND
DARK SHADES) • WHITE • BLACK

Disposable icing bags (3)

Couplers

Icing tips: #2, #5, #1

Squeeze bottle

Toothpicks

1 Scoop the darker electric yellow icing into a bag fitted with a #2 tip, and outline the starfish. A

2 Thin the lighter electric yellow icing for flooding (see page 16). Cover it with a damp dishtowel and let it sit for several minutes. Gently stir it with a silicone spatula and transfer it to a squeeze bottle.
→ Fill in the outlined areas with the thinned icing. Use a toothpick to guide icing to the edges and pop air bubbles. B
→ Let the cookies dry for at least one hour.

3 Pipe on the following details:
→ Use a #5 tip with white icing to add eyes.
→ Use a #2 tip with black icing to add pupils to the eyes.
→ Use a #1 tip with white icing to add detail to the eyes.
→ Use a #1 tip with black icing to pipe a smile. C

4 Use a #1 tip with the darker electric yellow icing to pipe dots on the arms of the starfish. D
→ Let the cookies dry uncovered for 6 to 8 hours or overnight.

Option: thin purple icing and add stripes on top if the yellow. For the method, see page 18.

OCTOPUSES

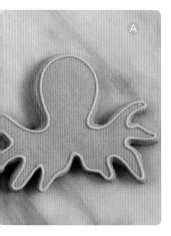
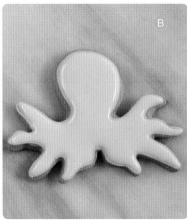

you will need

Pink Lemonade Cut-Out Cookies (page 27), octopus shape

Royal icing (page 29), divided and tinted:
ELECTRIC PINK (LIGHT AND DARK SHADES) • BLACK • WHITE

Disposable icing bags (3)

Couplers

Icing tips: #2, #5, #1

Squeeze bottle

Toothpicks

1 Scoop some of the darker electric pink icing into a bag fitted with a #2 tip, and outline the octopus. Ⓐ

2 Thin the lighter electric pink icing for flooding (see page 16). Cover it with a damp dishtowel and let it sit for several minutes. Gently stir it with a silicone spatula and transfer it to a squeeze bottle.
→ Fill in the outlined areas with the thinned icing. Use a toothpick to guide icing to the edges and pop air bubbles. Ⓑ
→ Let the cookies dry for at least one hour.

3 Pipe on the following details:
→ Use a #5 tip with white icing to add eyes.
→ Use a #2 tip with black icing to add pupils.
→ Use a #1 tip with white icing to add details to the eyes.
→ Use a #1 tip with black icing to add a smile. Ⓒ

4 Use a #1 tip with the darker electric pink icing to pipe small circles onto the arms of the octopus. Ⓓ

→ Let the cookies dry uncovered for 6 to 8 hours or overnight.

Option: thin yellow icing and add dots and lines on top of the pink. For method, see page 18.

JELLYFISH

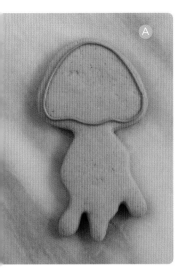
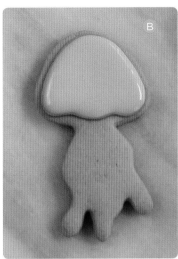

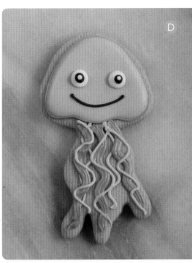

you will need

Pink Lemonade Cut-Out Cookies (page 27), jellyfish shape

Royal icing (page 29), divided and tinted:
PURPLE (LIGHT AND DARK SHADES) • BLACK • WHITE

Disposable icing bags (4)

Couplers

Icing tips: #2, #5, #1, small leaf tip

Squeeze bottle

Toothpicks

1 Scoop some of the dark purple icing into a bag fitted with a #2 tip, and outline the jellyfish. A

2 Reserve some light purple icing before thinning for piping details later. Thin the light purple icing for flooding (see page 16). Cover it with a damp dishtowel and let it sit for several minutes. Gently stir it with a silicone spatula and transfer it to a squeeze bottle.
→ Fill in the outlined areas with the thinned icing. Use a toothpick to guide icing to the edges and pop air bubbles. B
→ Let the cookies dry for at least one hour.

3 Pipe on the following details:
→ Use a #5 tip with white icing to add eyes.
→ Use a #2 tip with black icing to add pupils.
→ Use a #1 tip with white icing to add details to the eyes.
→ Use a #1 tip with black icing to add a smile. C

4 Use a #1 tip with light purple icing to pipe squiggly lines down from the body.
→ Use a small leaf tip with dark purple icing to add larger squiggly lines that overlap the thinner ones. Add a few more thin lines on top. D
→ Let the cookies dry uncovered for 6 to 8 hours or overnight.

Option: thin pink icing and drop dots on top of the purple. For an example, see photo on page 18.

FISH

you will need

Pink Lemonade Cut-Out Cookies (page 27), fish shape

Royal icing (page 29), divided and tinted:
ELECTRIC GREEN (LIGHT AND DARK SHADES) • WHITE • BLACK

Disposable icing bags (3)

Couplers

Icing tips: #2, #5, #1

Squeeze bottle

Toothpicks

1 Scoop some of the dark electric green icing into a bag fitted with a #2 tip, and outline the fish. A

2 Thin the lighter electric green icing for flooding (see page 16). Cover it with a damp dishtowel and let it sit for several minutes. Gently stir it with a silicone spatula and transfer it to a squeeze bottle.
→ Fill in the outlined areas with the thinned icing. Use a toothpick to guide the icing to the edges and pop air bubbles. B
→ Let the cookies dry for at least one hour.

3 Pipe on the following details:
→ Use a #5 tip with white icing to add eyes.
→ Use a #2 tip with black icing to add pupils.
→ Use a #1 tip with white icing to details to the eyes. C

4 Use a #1 tip with the darker electric green icing to add detailing to the fish. D
→ Let the cookies dry uncovered for 6 to 8 hours or overnight.

Option: thin blue icing and drop lines across the green icing. Run a toothpick through the lines to marble (see page 18 for method).

SEA HORSES

you will need

Pink Lemonade Cut-Out Cookies
(page 27), sea horse shape

Royal icing (page 29),
divided and tinted:
ELECTRIC BLUE (LIGHT AND
DARK SHADES) • WHITE • BLACK

Disposable icing bags (3)

Couplers

Icing tips: #2, #5, #1

Squeeze bottles (2)

Toothpicks

1 Scoop some of the dark electric blue icing into a bag fitted with a #2 tip, and outline the starfish. Section off an area for a fin. A

2 Thin both of the blue icings for flooding (see on page 16). Cover them with a damp dishtowel and let them sit for several minutes. Gently stir them with a silicone spatula and transfer them to squeeze bottles.
→ Fill in the outlined areas with the thinned icing, flooding the fin with the darker electric blue icing. Use a toothpick to guide icing to the edges and pop air bubbles. B
→ Let the cookies dry for at least one hour.

3 Pipe on the following details:
→ Use a #5 tip with white icing to add eyes.
→ Use a #2 tip with black icing to add pupils.
→ Use a #1 tip with white icing to add details to the eyes. C
→ Use a #1 tip with the darker electric blue icing to add dots to the belly of the sea horse, and add detail to the fin. D
→ Let the cookies dry uncovered for 6 to 8 hours or overnight.

Option: thin electric green icing and add scalloped lines across the blue icing. For method see page 18.

BABY SHOWER

With their bright primary colors and vintage shapes, these cookies will add nostalgia and whimsy to your next baby shower. Put the cookies in individual bags, tie them with ribbons, and you've got perfect shower favors. You can also group them together on a platter for a delicious dessert-table centerpiece.

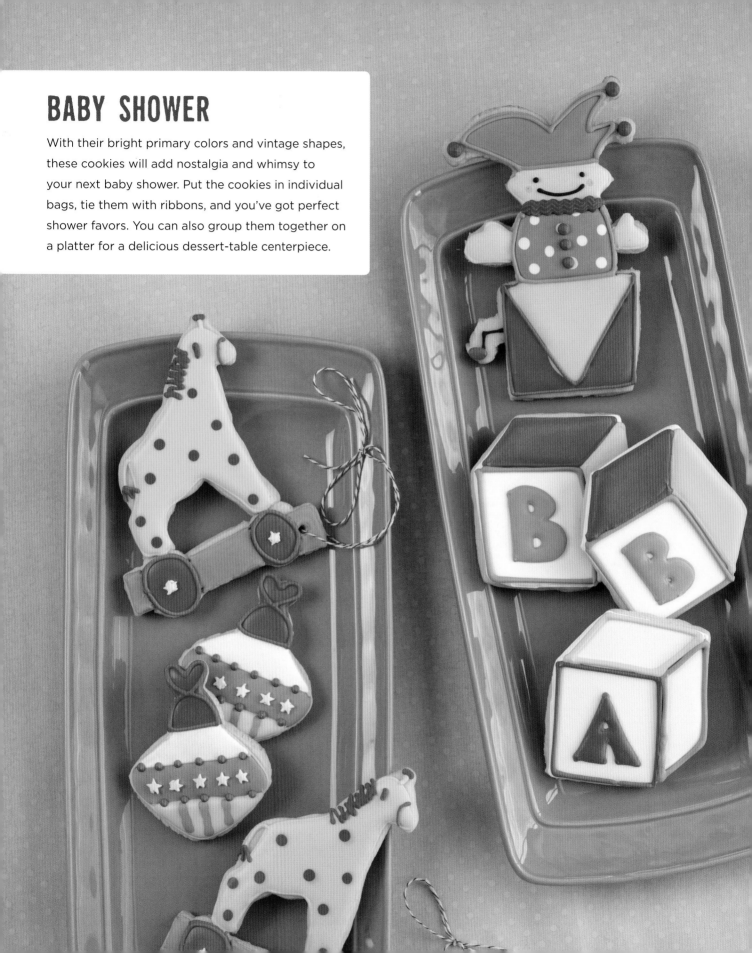

BLOCKS

you will need

Vanilla-Almond Sugar Cookies
(page 24), toy block shape

Royal icing (page 29),
divided and tinted:
WHITE • RED • ROYAL BLUE •
YELLOW

Disposable icing bags (4)

Couplers

Icing tips: #2, #3

Squeeze bottles (4)

Toothpicks

1 Scoop some white icing into a bag fitted with a #2 tip, and
outline the cookies.

2 Thin the white icing for flooding (as described on page 16). Cover
it with a damp dishtowel and let it sit for several minutes. Gently stir
it with a silicone spatula and transfer it to a squeeze bottle.
→ Fill in the outlined areas with the thinned icing. Use a toothpick
to guide the icing to the edges and pop air bubbles. Ⓐ
→ Let the cookies dry for at least one hour.

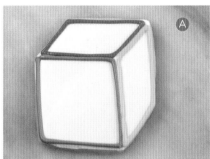

3 Using a #3 tip with the red or royal blue icings, pipe
the outline for the front of the block.
→ Use a #3 tip with the red, royal blue, and yellow icings to outline
the remaining sides.

4 Use a #2 tip with red or blue icing to pipe the outline of a letter. Ⓑ

5 Thin the red, royal blue, and yellow icings for flooding (see page
16). Cover them with a damp dishtowel and let them sit for several
minutes. Gently stir them with a silicone spatula and transfer them
to squeeze bottles as needed.
→ Fill in the outlined areas with the thinned icing. Use a toothpick
to guide the icing to the edges and pop air bubbles. Ⓒ
→ Let the cookies dry uncovered for 6 to 8 hours or overnight.

Variation: On some blocks, leave the outlines unfilled.

JACK-IN-THE-BOXES

you will need

Vanilla-Almond Sugar Cookies (page 24), jack-in-the-box shape (template on page 143)

Royal icing (page 29), divided and tinted:
ROYAL BLUE • COPPER • RED • YELLOW • WHITE • BLACK

Disposable icing bags (4)

Couplers

Icing tips: #2, #1, small star or French tip

Squeeze bottles (5)

Toothpicks

Pink food coloring pen

1 Scoop the royal blue icing into a bag fitted with a #2 tip, and outline the hat and shirt. Reserve some of this icing in the bag for piping details later. Ⓐ

2 Pipe on the following outlines:
→ Use a #2 tip with copper icing to outline the face and arms.
→ Use a #2 tip with red icing to outline the box. Reserve some of this icing in the bag for piping details later. Ⓑ

3 Thin the royal blue, coppe, red, yellow, and white icings for flooding (see page 16). Cover them with a damp dishtowel and let them sit for several minutes. Gently stir them with a silicone spatula and transfer them to squeeze bottles as needed.
→ Fill in the outlined areas with the thinned icing. Use a toothpick to guide the icing to the edges and pop air bubbles.
→ Using the flood-on-flood method described on page 18, drop dots of white icing onto the wet blue base of the shirt. Wait several minutes for the base color to set before you add the white dots. Ⓒ
→ Let the cookies dry for at least one hour.

4 Use a #1 tip with black icing to add eyes, a mouth, and a handle.

5 Use a small star or French tip with red icing to pipe the neck ruffle, using a back-and-forth motion. The icing will need to be stiff to hold the lines from the tip, so practice on a paper towel first. Ⓓ
→ Use a #2 tip red icing to outline the box.

6 Squeeze the red icing back into a bowl and add a few drops of water. The icing should still be of piping consistency, but it shouldn't peak when a dot is piped. Test the icing by pushing a little of it through a tip before you transfer it back to the piping bag.
→ Use a #2 tip with red icing to add dots for buttons on the hat, the shirt, and at the end of the handle.
→ Use a #2 tip with royal blue icing to outline the hat and the shirt.
→ Let the cookies dry uncovered for 6 to 8 hours or overnight.

7 When the cookies are dry, add cheeks with the pink food coloring pen. Ⓔ

TOPS

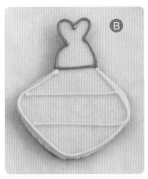

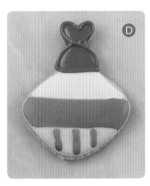
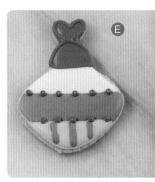

you will need

Vanilla-Almond Sugar Cookies (page 24), toy top shape (template on page 143)

Royal icing (page 29), divided and tinted:
RED • YELLOW • WHITE • ROYAL BLUE

Disposable icing bags (2)

Couplers

Icing tips: #2, #1

Squeeze bottles (4)

Toothpicks

Tweezers

Star sprinkles

1 Scoop some red icing into a bag fitted with a #2 tip, and outline the handle of the top. Reserve some of this icing in the bag for piping details later. Ⓐ

2 Scoop some yellow icing into a bag, attach a #2 tip, and outline the rest of the top, sectioning off an area across the middle. Ⓑ

3 Thin the red, yellow, white, and royal blue icings for flooding (see page 16). Cover them with a damp dishtowel and let them sit for several minutes. Gently stir them with a silicone spatula and transfer them to squeeze bottles as needed.
→ Fill in the red outlined areas with the red thinned icing, and the center area with blue. Fill in the top section with white icing. Use a toothpick to guide the icing to the edges and pop air bubbles.

4 Using the flood-on-flood method described on page 18, fill in the bottom outline with the thinned yellow icing. Use a toothpick to guide the icing to the edges and pop air bubbles.

5 Using a squeeze bottle fitted with a small tip, squeeze vertical lines of thinned royal blue icing across the bottom yellow section of the top. Leave them as stripes or drag a toothpick across them for a marbled look. Ⓒ
→ Let the cookies dry for at least one hour.

6 Use a #2 tip with red icing to pipe an outline of the top handle over the flood icing. Ⓓ

7 Squeeze the red icing back into a bowl and add a few drops of water. The icing should still be of piping consistency, but it shouldn't peak when a dot is piped. Test the icing by pushing a little of it through a tip before you transfer it back to the piping bag.
→ Use a #2 tip with red icing to pipe small dots along the edges of the blue area. Ⓔ
→ Let the cookies dry uncovered for 6 to 8 hours or overnight.

8 Use a #1 tip to pipe small dots of white icing across the center of the top. Use tweezers to place star sprinkles onto the dots of icing.

GIRAFFE PULL-TOY

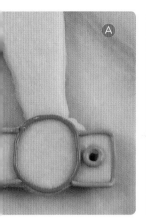  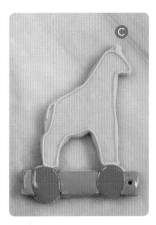 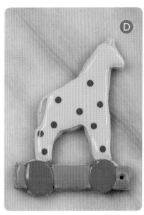 

you will need

Vanilla-Almond Sugar Cookies (page 24), giraffe pull-toy (see Note)

Royal icing (page 29), divided and tinted:
RED • ROYAL BLUE • YELLOW • BROWN • WHITE

Disposable icing bags (5)

Couplers

Icing tips: #2, #1

Squeeze bottles (4)

Toothpicks

Tweezers

Star sprinkles

Baker's twine

Note: This cookie is made by combining a giraffe cut-out with the rolling base template on page 143. Position the two pieces next to each other on the cookie sheet, and they'll bake as one piece. As soon as the batch comes out of the oven, use a toothpick to poke a hole all the way through one end of each cookie for threading the baker's twine.

1 Scoop some red icing into a bag fitted with a #2 tip, and outline the wheels. Reserve some of this icing in the bag for piping details later.
→ Scoop some royal blue icing into a bag, attach a #2 tip, and outline the base of the toy. Pipe around the hole you made for the string so it doesn't fill with icing. Ⓐ

2 Scoop some yellow icing into a bag, attach a #2 tip, and outline the giraffe. Pipe the giraffe's horn and tail. Ⓑ
→ Reserve a bit of brown icing for piping details before you thin it. Thin the red, blue, yellow, and brown icings for flooding (see page 16). Cover them with a damp dishtowel and let them sit for several minutes. Gently stir them with a silicone spatula and transfer them to squeeze bottles as needed.
→ Fill the red and blue cookie outlines with the thinned icing. Use a toothpick to guide the icing to the edges and pop air bubbles. Ⓒ

3 Using the flood-on-flood method described on page 18, fill the giraffe with the thinned yellow icing. Use a toothpick to guide the icing to the edges and pop air bubbles. Drop dots of thinned brown icing onto the body of the giraffe. Ⓓ
→ Let the cookies dry for at least one hour.

4 Use a #2 tip with red icing to pipe over the outline of the wheels.
→ Use a #1 tip with brown icing to pipe details on the face, neck, horn, and tail of the giraffe. Ⓔ
→ Let the cookies dry uncovered for 6 to 8 hours or overnight.

5 Use a #1 tip to pipe a dot of white icing onto the center of each wheel. Use tweezers to place a star sprinkle onto the dots of icing.

6 When the cookies are dry, thread pieces of baker's twine through their holes.

WEDDING/BRIDAL SHOWER

Bring an extra bit of bliss to a bridal shower, engagement
party, or wedding reception with these delightful cookies.
They're double-deckers, which means they're twice as fun—
and twice as delicious—as regular cut-outs.

BASE COOKIES

you will need

Vanilla-Almond Sugar Cookies
(page 24), scalloped oval shape

Royal icing (page 29),
divided and tinted:
PINK (LIGHT AND DARK SHADES)

Disposable icing bags (2)

Couplers

Icing tips: #2

Squeeze bottles (2)

Toothpicks

1 Scoop some light pink icing into a bag fitted with a #2 tip, and outline half of the base cookies. Repeat, except using dark pink icing. Reserve some of the pink icings in the bags for piping details later.
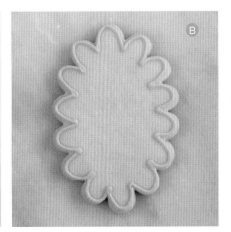 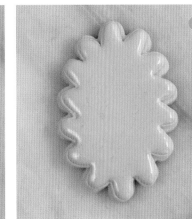
Ⓐ and Ⓑ

2 Thin both of the pink icings for flooding (see page 16). Cover them with a damp dishtowel and let them sit for several minutes. Gently stir them with a silicone spatula and transfer them to squeeze bottles as needed.
→ Fill in the outlined areas with the light pink and dark pink icings. Use a toothpick to guide the icing to the edges and pop air bubbles.
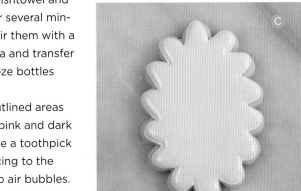
Ⓒ and Ⓓ

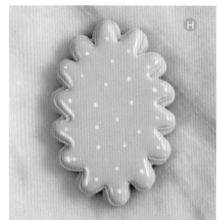

3 Using the flood-on-flood method described on page 18, squeeze lines of contrasting light pink and dark pink icing onto one-third of the batch of cookies. (E) and (F)

4 Use a toothpick to add tiny dots to another third of the batch: Dip the toothpick into the contrasting color of pink flood icing and place it directly on the base color. (G) and (H)

5 Leave the remaining third of the batch of cookies solid.
→ Let the cookies dry uncovered for 6 to 8 hours or overnight.

6 To assemble a mini top cookie to the base cookie:
→ Pipe a bit of icing onto the back of each mini cookie. Place the ring-shaped mini cookies on top of the striped base cookies, the cake-shaped mini cookies on top of the solid base cookies, and the bouquet-shaped mini cookies on top of the dotted base cookies.
→ Let the cookies dry for one hour before packaging or storing.

RINGS

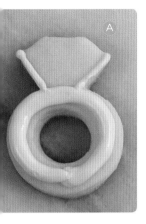
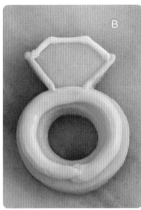

you will need

Vanilla-Almond Sugar Cookies (page 24), mini ring shape

Royal Icing (page 29), divided and tinted:
YELLOW • WHITE

Disposable icing bags (2)

Couplers

Icing tips: #5, #2, #1

Squeeze bottle

Toothpicks

Meringue powder

Small paintbrushes

Rainbow disco dust

Vodka

Gold luster dust

1 Scoop some yellow icing into a bag fitted with a #5 tip, and pipe a circle for the ring.
➜ Switch to a #2 tip and pipe prongs on each side of the ring. Ⓐ

2 Scoop some white icing into a bag, attach a #2 tip, and pipe the diamond outline. Reserve some of this icing in the bag for piping details later. Ⓑ

3 Thin the white icing for flooding (see page 16). Cover it with a damp dishtowel and let it sit for several minutes. Gently stir it with a silicone spatula and transfer it to a squeeze bottle.
➜ Fill in each diamond with the thinned icing. Use a toothpick to guide the icing to the edges and pop air bubbles. Ⓒ
➜ Let the cookies dry for at least 30 minutes.

4 Use a #1 tip with white icing to add details to the diamond. Ⓓ
➜ Let the cookies dry uncovered for 6 to 8 hours or overnight.

5 When the cookies are dry, mix together equal amounts of meringue powder and water. Apply the mixture to the ring detail piping with a small paintbrush. Sprinkle on the disco dust. Use a dry brush to remove the excess.

6 Mix ¼ teaspoon gold luster dust with several drops of vodka until smooth. Use a paintbrush to apply the mixture to the ring and prongs. Ⓔ

7 See page 22 for instructions on adhering mini cookies to base cookies.

BOUQUETS

you will need

Vanilla-Almond Sugar Cookies (page 24), mini bouquet shape (made with a cherry cookie cutter)

Royal Icing (page 29), divided and tinted: PINK (LIGHT AND DARK SHADES) • YELLOW • TURQUOISE • GREEN

Disposable icing bags (5)

Couplers

Icing tips: #3, #1

1 Scoop some light pink icing into a bag fitted with a #3 tip, and pipe the bases for swirly roses. Ⓐ

2 Scoop some dark pink icing into a bag, attach a #1 tip, and pipe a swirl on top of each base. Ⓑ

3 Use a #1 tip with yellow icing to pipe on five-petaled flowers.
→ Use a #1 tip with dark pink icing to add centers to the flowers. Ⓒ

4 Use a #1 tip with turquoise icing to fill in the bouquet with dots. Ⓓ

5 Use a #1 tip with green icing to add the stems. Ⓔ
→ Let the cookies dry uncovered for 6 to 8 hours or overnight.

6 Use a #1 tip with light pink icing to add a ribbon to each bouquet stem.

7 See page 22 for instructions on adhering mini cookies to base cookies.

CAKES

 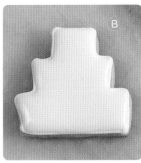 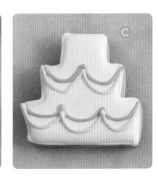  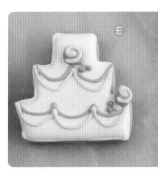

you will need

Vanilla-Almond Sugar Cookies (page 24), mini cake shape

Royal icing (page 29), divided and tinted:
WHITE • PINK (LIGHT AND DARK SHADES) • YELLOW • TURQUOISE

Disposable icing bags (5)

Couplers

Icing tips: #2, #1, #3

Squeeze bottle

Toothpicks

1 Scoop some white icing into a bag fitted with a #2 tip, and outline the cookies. Ⓐ

2 Thin the white icing for flooding (see page 16). Cover it with a damp dishtowel and let it sit for several minutes. Gently stir it with a silicone spatula and transfer it to a squeeze bottle as needed.
→ Fill in the outlined areas with the thinned icing. Use a toothpick to guide the icing to the edges and pop air bubbles. Ⓑ
→ Let the cookies dry for at least 30 minutes.

3 On half of the cookies, use #1 tips with the light and dark pink icings to pipe swags. Ⓒ

4 Use a #3 tip with dark pink icing to pipe the base of a swirly rose.
→ Use a #1 tip with contrasting pink icing to add a swirl to the top of the base. Ⓓ

5 Use #1 tips with yellow and turquoise icings to add small dots next to the roses. Ⓔ

6 On the remaining cookies (see below), create a cluster of swirly roses in one corner: Use #3 tips with one of the pink icings to pipe the base of a swirly rose. Use a #1 tip to pipe a swirl in contrasting pink on top of the base. Ⓕ

7 Use #1 tips with yellow and turquoise icings to pipe small dots next to the roses. Ⓖ
→ Let the cookies dry uncovered for 6 to 8 hours or overnight.

8 See page 22 for instructions on adhering mini cookies to base cookies.

ABOUT THE AUTHOR

Bridget Edwards has been decorating cookies for more than a decade and eating them for as long as she can remember. A self-taught cookie decorator, she started the blog Bake at 350 in 2007 so that she could share her secrets for making beautifully decorated cookies. Bridget's cookies have been featured on MarthaStewart.com, bonappetit.com, and the *Houston Chronicle*. Her blog, Bake at 350, was nominated as a top five baking blog by *Better Homes and Gardens*. In addition to blogging, she also develops recipes for Imperial Sugar. Bridget's first book, *Decorating Cookies*, was published by Lark in 2012. She lives in Texas with her husband, son, and two kitties. Visit her blog at bakeat350.blogspot.com.

ACKNOWLEDGMENTS

Mark and Jack: You are the loves of my life. Thank you for being my recipe testers, design consultants, and mistake eaters. I promise the dining room table won't be covered with cookies forever.

Mom and Dad: Thank you for raising me in a house where the food was delicious, fun, never too fancy, and meant to be shared. Dad, your support means more to me than you know. Mom, I miss you every day.

Molly: You're the most thoughtful sister a girl could ask for. Thank you.

Mac: Thanks for the seahorse-cookie inspiration!

Uncle Mike: Thank you for encouraging me, sharing your business savvy, and always remembering mom.

TERESA!: Yes, your name is in all caps. Thank you for everything...mostly our text conversations about important world issues, like lipstick and sprinkles.

Lupita: I'm so happy you're in my life! Thank you for your love and enthusiasm (and your beautiful cookies)!

Amy, Wendy, Ree, Sandy, Rebecca, and Robyn: We've laughed. We've cried. We've made cheese. I treasure your friendship!

The Ya-Ya's: Thank you for being a second (crazy) family.

Claudia, Alisa, Karen, Kristen, Ann, Beverly, and Lupita: You guys are the sweetest friends! Let's decorate cookies together again soon! Next time...no photography, and maybe wine?

Sara: For the French lessons, merci!

Haydar, Greg, Jenny, and the Hubbell & Hudson crew: Thank you for letting us have a cookie party in the Cooking School! We loved every minute!

Angie: I think I speak for all makers of sweet treats... your inspiration knows no bounds.

Linda & Kristi: Thank you for your devoting your time and creative talents to all things cookie!

Beth: I'll always remember your first email. Thanks for getting me started on this path!

The food/craft/home blogging community: The creativity, passion, and talent that you bring to your blogs inspire me each and every day. Many of you are not only blogging friends, you're real-life friends (and fellow troublemakers). You know who you are, and I love you to pieces.

The readers of Bake at 350: Thank you from the bottom of my heart for reading my rambling blog stories and baking along with me! I love you for supporting my cookie habit. Yay, cookies!

TEMPLATES

Enlarge templates 200%

EYEGLASSES
BOOK CLUB
page 47

GIRAFFE PULL-TOY
BABY SHOWER
page 130

METEORS
OUTER SPACE
page 86

JACK-IN-THE-BOXES
BABY SHOWER
page 126

TOPS
BABY SHOWER
page 128

RESOURCES

INDEX

DECORATING
COOKIES
PARTY